TENDING THE GARDEN

ESSAYS ON THE GOSPEL AND THE EARTH

Edited by
Wesley Granberg-Michaelson

WILLIAM B. EERDMANS PUBLISHING COMPANY
GRAND RAPIDS, MICHIGAN

Copyright © 1987 by Wm. B. Eerdmans Publishing Co.
255 Jefferson Ave. S.E., Grand Rapids, Mich. 49503
Printed in the United States of America

Library of Congress Cataloging-in-Publication Data:

Tending the garden.

1. Nature--Religious aspects--Christianity.
2. Human ecology--Religious aspects--Christianity.
I. Granberg-Michaelson, Wesley.
BT695.5.T46   1986   231.7   86-29236

ISBN 0-8028-0230-3

Contents

v

Preface

The essays in this volume comprise a wellspring of rich biblical insight and creative theological work concerning the relationship of God, humanity, and all creation. The gathering of this reservoir of Christian insight has been made possible by the AuSable Institute. Located in the northern part of Michigan's lower peninsula, the AuSable Institute is a unique resource for training Christians about their relationship to the environment.

The philosophy of the AuSable Institute reads in part as follows: "The Board, faculty, and staff of the AuSable Institute confess that God is owner of all. Humankind is not the owner of that over which it has authority. Human authority is more that of trustee than owner. The scope of this trust is global. Since all creatures depend on the earth for life, health, and fulfillment, stewardship is the responsible use and care of creation. This is a clear and repeated testimony of Scripture." Graced with such a philosophy, AuSable defines its mission in this manner: "The mission of the AuSable Institute is to be a center for study and experiences which integrate environmental information with Christian thought for the purpose of bringing the Christian community and the general public to a better understanding of the Creator and the stewardship of his creation. Therefore all of its programs and activities are conducted for the promotion of Christian environmental stewardship, both in operation and in the plans and programs it develops, promotes and maintains."

Central to the task of AuSable Institute has been the training of students from Christian colleges, who come for a quarter of study to gain greater ecological knowledge and training in order to be stewards of the creation. In addition, since 1980, the Au-

Sable Institute has held a yearly forum that brings together church leaders, educators, experts in the environmental sciences, theologians, activists, and others to discuss specific themes concerning biblical stewardship of the environment. Such a forum provided the context for many of the essays in this book. (Further information concerning the AuSable Institute can be provided by writing them at RR #2, Mancelona, Michigan 49659.)

Thanks goes to each of the authors whose work is represented in this volume, but special thanks is also due to Dr. Calvin DeWitt, Director of the AuSable Institute; Bob Barr, Coordinator of Support Services at AuSable; and the entire Board of the Institute, who have supported the forums each year, and thus also make possible the publication of this volume.

Sharon Murfin, Administrative Assistant at the New Creation Institute in Missoula, Montana, has been an indispensable help in coordinating the correspondence and work that has shaped this book.

Finally, I wish to thank Jon Pott, Editor-in-Chief at Eerdmans Publishing Company, who has consistently believed in the value of this publication.

WESLEY GRANBERG-MICHAELSON

Introduction:
Identification or Mastery?

Wesley Granberg-Michaelson

In 1938 the famous missionary John R. Mott was in India to attend a world missionary conference. While there, he paid a visit to Sevegram, the home of Mahatma Gandhi. During the course of their conversation Mott asked Gandhi, "What do you want to achieve in this world?" Gandhi replied simply, "To identify myself with all creation." Mott left the encounter theologically disappointed.

Like many parents of pre-school children, I try to censor what my son and daughter watch on television. One of those children's programs I ban is the cartoon called "He-Man and the Masters of the Universe." But the program is highly popular. This television series chronicles for the child's imagination the adventures of superhumans battling to achieve militaristic mastery over their mythical universe. Many families with youngsters captivated by this program have spent as much as several hundred dollars on all the various toys, games, and clothes that further carry out the program's theme.

The tension between identifying with the creation and achieving mastery over it is ageless. But in more modern times the scientific revolution fundamentally changed humanity's relationship to the creation. With the wedding of science and technology and the reshaping of life through the Industrial Revolution, Western culture has firmly entrenched the idea of human mastery over the creation rather than identification with it. Rebellions against this dominant mold—such as the romantic period and, later, existentialism—have been put down. Science and technology have been welcomed as the conquerors of the creation. The steam engine, the development of plastics, atomic energy, the transistor, the modern computer, biotechnology—all

1

have been hailed as marvelous new technological solutions to pressing problems.

Undeniably, technological breakthroughs like these and many others have dramatically transformed modern life and have contributed much to human betterment. Yet such developments always bring with them a host of related new problems. Technological accomplishments create new dangers.

Within the last two decades, humanity's mastery over the creation has begun to be questioned simply on the basis of the effects of that mastery on the creation. Many trace the beginning of the modern environmental movement to the publication of Rachel Carson's *Silent Spring* in 1962. Since that time, a broad public movement has gained widespread political power, has spawned myriad laws, regulations, and litigation, and has alerted the world's political consciousness. Yet the threats to the integrity of the life-supporting resources of the creation—its water, air, land, and sources of energy—have seemed to accelerate even while the environmental movement has gained momentum. And while other modern movements of social conscience have been strengthened and even motivated by the church, the environmental movement is a clear exception to this pattern.

Until recent years, the church has been notably uninvolved with the task of serving God's creation. Many environmental critics, in fact, charge that the church has justified and perpetuated humanity's stance as the ruthless master of the creation. At least since the Reformation, Western Christianity has been quick to stress humanity's role to "rule over and subdue" the earth, providing a godly rationale for the onslaughts of modern technology and offering few if any safeguards against the desecration of the earth.

Calvin DeWitt, Director of the AuSable Institute, an evangelically based education center for promoting Christian stewardship of the earth, has marshaled evidence indicating the church's negative impact on its own members regarding their stance toward the creation. DeWitt points to the findings of Stephen Kellert, Associate Professor of Forestry at Yale University, who did a lengthy survey of human attitudes toward nature and wildlife. Kellert devised a scale of eight attitudes toward animals ranging between identification and mastery: naturalistic, ecologistic, humanistic, moralistic, scientistic, utilitarian, dominionistic, and negativistic. Using elaborate questionnaires, he surveyed a diverse number of people in order to discover the range and strength of these various views toward the animal world. He then correlated these attitudes with a variety of demographic and descriptive characteristics. One of these happened to be the frequency of attendance at religious services.

Statistically, the discovery was rather startling. The more frequently an individual attended religious services, the higher the probability that his or her attitudes toward animals would tend toward those of dominion or even outright negativity. Similarly, those who reported that they rarely (if ever) attended religious services were far more likely to display an ecological or naturalistic stance toward the animal world. DeWitt's point, of course, is that such statistical findings simply underscore the urgent need for the church to teach its members proper biblical stewardship of God's creation.

That task requires a new look at the Bible and a fresh perspective for theology. Since the Reformation, the Protestant church of the West has been theologically preoccupied with the questions of God's relationship to humanity. For a variety of reasons, the creation has simply been dropped out of the theological equation. But in recent times, new biblical study and attention to the threats facing the earth have prompted a slow but growing rediscovery of the creation as a fundamental theme for biblical theology.

The Bible simply makes more sense when we recognize that it is the story of how God, humanity, and the creation relate to each other. The Bible offers the modern age a rich reservoir of insight concerning humanity's relationship to the creation, and the relationship of both to God. Such wisdom is essential in order to save the creation from the peril of destruction that it presently faces. Of course, hearing fresh biblical words about the creation's relationship to God and to humanity will raise certain questions.

First, does the Bible grant humanity unchallenged dominion over the creation? For the past three hundred years the Western church has rarely if ever doubted this assumption. However, clear biblical study offered by several authors in this book makes it evident that the Bible says something quite different. It does not grant humankind permission to take the earth into their own hands and use it to suit their own selfish purposes. In fact, that is what the Bible prohibits and defines as sin. Rather, the Bible sees the nature of humanity's dominion as service for the sake of all creation.

The second question that arises has to do with priorities. Aren't spiritual realities ultimately more important than material things, including the earth? The Bible fights against the kind of dualism that modern Christians want to read into its pages. It may seem convenient to divide reality into spirit and flesh, soul and body, heaven and earth, mind and matter, or good and evil. But the Bible sees things as one whole. Specifically, the physical nature of the creation not only is affirmed as good but cannot be divorced from spiritual realities. That is why Christ took on flesh and blood, why he entered into the physical world and became part of it. His rising from the grave was a resurrection of both spirit and body. God's spirit "renews the face of the earth" (Ps. 104:30).

The third question has to do with the presumed temporality of the creation. Isn't creation headed for destruction at the end of time? Christians have always found it easy to believe that God will save them, but they find it more difficult to believe that God's intention is to save and restore the whole creation. Yet this is the constant declaration of the Word of God. God's redemption reaches out to his creation. And this new creation that we are introduced to in Christ is not one that awaits us at the end of time but that, like the resurrection of our Lord, has already broken into history.

Clearly, the Bible's picture of the intended relationship of God, humanity, and the created world presents us with fresh challenges for understanding and living out our faith. Our basic doctrines of creation, the Fall, the Incarnation, and redemption need to be considered in this light, and several authors in this book provide extremely useful and discerning insight in so doing.

In this theological journey, resources new yet ancient will be of particular help. Two deserve special mention. The first is the theology and tradition of the Eastern Orthodox Church. This branch of Christianity has for too long been neglected and ignored by many Christians in the West. Its theological perspectives offer enriching truths concerning the Bible's understanding of God's relationship to the creation. The wisdom literature within the Bible likewise provides us with much-needed help and perspective on these questions. Recent Old Testament study has helped shed light on much of Scripture by explaining this school of thought and practice present within the faith of Israel. One of the practical benefits to be gained from examining this resource will be concrete guidance in constructing a Christian ethic toward the environment.

In John 6:51 Christ declares, "The bread which I shall give for the life of the world is my flesh." Today the church is challenged anew to understand and live out the truth of such a declaration. Christ's life gives life not only to believers but to the whole world, to the cosmos. And that which gives life to the world is rooted in Christ's own body—his flesh. The Incarnation testifies that God takes on physical form and life. This means that all of creation awaits transformation through the life of Christ. And the church, which is now Christ's body on earth, is to be the sign of that transformation already taking root.

The Bible prohibits us from reducing Christ to a purely spiritual force, just as it refuses to limit Christ's effect to only our individual lives. Jesus Christ came in the flesh in order to give life to the world. All the authors in this book bear testimony to this truth. Our hope is that the life and witness of the church today may indeed be a sign that the new creation has already dawned.

New Age, New Consciousness, and the New Creation

Loren Wilkinson

The AuSable Trails Institute for Environmental Studies in Mancelona, Michigan, was once a Christian camp which, perhaps through a divine sense of humor, discovered in the early seventies that it was situated over a large deposit of oil. Some people of great vision saw the value of using the income from that resource to set up a Christian study center devoted to looking at how, as Christians, we use our resources. It was, and is, a remarkable vision, but it is interesting to speculate where the money might have gone if the oil had been discovered even a few years earlier and the income from it had been at the disposal of a similarly responsible and dedicated group of Christians.

Twenty-five years ago, there were no environmental studies institutes, Christian or otherwise. Ecology was an obscure branch of biology, not a household cliché. Among Christians, "stewardship" meant sermons on tithing. "Organic" referred either to a particularly difficult branch of chemistry or to the obsession of a few health-food fanatics. To the popular mind at least,

LOREN WILKINSON *is Associate Professor of Interdisciplinary Studies and Philosophy at Regent College in Vancouver, British Columbia. Previously he taught at the Oregon Extension of Trinity College in Deerfield, Illinois. Professor Wilkinson brings together a rare mixture of interest and involvement in the sciences and the arts. He has been involved in organizing Christian arts festivals in the Vancouver area, and he is also active in the Institute for Public Discipleship, an adjunct of Regent College that speaks to social issues. He edited the book* Earthkeeping: Christian Stewardship of Natural Resources *(Eerdmans, 1980), which has been very influential in developing a theology of creation.*

energy seemed cheap and inexhaustible, the world economy liable to build and grow forever. There was no such thing as "the Third World"—only developed and underdeveloped nations—and it was the good fortune of the underdeveloped nations to have the developed nations rapidly developing them for everyone's mutual benefit.

Many of these ideas are still current, both in the Christian church and in culture at large. Nevertheless, an enormous change has come over the cultural landscape. Today, phrases like "environmental crisis," "ecological awareness," and "stewardship of the earth's resources" have entered the popular vocabulary not only of Western culture but of evangelical Christianity.

Why bother to point this out? For one very important reason. The attempts by Christians to formulate a Christian environmental ethic are for the most part following, not setting, a general cultural trend. True, much has been written about sources in Scripture and in the Christian tradition that would nourish a kind of theology of the earth. But all these attempts to develop an environmental ethic based on the Bible and drawing on various resources in the Christian tradition—from Saint Francis to Eastern Orthodoxy to Anabaptism to Kuyperian Calvinism—*are part of a cultural and religious movement that is much larger than Christianity itself.*

Let me illustrate my point by taking you to a bookstore not far from where I live in Vancouver, British Columbia. It is one of the best places to buy a variety of books that deal with the ethical dimensions of our life on the planet. All of the environmentalist saints are here, old and new—from Saint Francis to Thoreau to Aldo Leopold to Wendell Berry and E. F. Schumacher. We find such books as Hazel Henderson's *Politics of the Solar Age: The Alternative to Economics,* Jonathan Schell's *Fate of the Earth,* and a large collection of books on appropriate technology, solar architecture, organic gardening, and so forth. More philosophical works are there as well: Carolyn Merchant's *Death in Nature,* J. E. Lovelock's *Gaia,* Gregory Bateson's *Steps to an Ecology of Mind,* and so on.

The bookstore—Banyen Books, it is called—is comfortable and well-lighted, finished in natural wood and softened with hanging plants. There are places to sit and read, and music—like Paul Winter's sax-accompanied wolf songs—is piped throughout. But the familiar books whose titles I've been quoting, like the books others have written in recent attempts to formulate a Christian environmentalist ethic, are embedded in a matrix of quite another kind of book.

Much of the store's inventory deals with a variety of Oriental religions. The books exploring them have titles like *The Teachings of Sri Ranakrishna*, *I Am God*, *Enlightenment without God*, and *Buddha in the Palm of Your Hand*. There is a large section on Taoism that includes books like *The Taoist Inner View of the Universe and the Immortal Realm*. There's also a large section on astrology and the occult that features titles like *Relationships and Life Cycles: Modern Dimensions of Astrology* and *Saturn: A New Look at an Old Devil*. There's *The Cosmic Informer: An Astrological Guide to Self-Discovery*. There's a large section on hallucinogenic drugs—books like *The Wonderous Mushroom* and *LSD: The Age of Mind*. There's a lot of material on the human potentials movement, with works by Theodore Reich, works about the Essalen Institute, books with titles like *The Owner's Manual for Your Life* and even crasser titles like *How to Have More in a Have-Not World* and *Wishcraft: How to Get What You Really Want*. *The Metaphysics of Sex* is there, along with *Sexual Spirituality*.

There are a lot of books about modern science, especially the philosophical dimensions of biology and physics. There are many books on the idea of changing paradigms, with Thomas Kuhn's *Structure of Scientific Revolutions* given a prominent place. There's also—tucked into one corner—a section on Christianity that offers several versions of the Bible and works by many writers in the tradition of Christian mysticism such as Meister Eckhart and Saint John of the Cross.

Banyen Books is like many bookstores I've been in. (Many natural food stores have the same atmosphere.) It's a religious bookstore of sorts, but it's more of a religious smorgasbord. It's not pushing any single religion but is rather bewilderingly eclectic. For Banyen Books and other bookstores like it (as well as such established countercultural bibles as *The Whole Earth Catalog*) cater not to people of any particular movement but to all those who find a harmony among the subjects from which I have listed some titles. And what is that harmony in which solar energy, organic farming, Zen meditation, altered states of consciousness, the metaphysics of sex, and Saint Francis of Assisi all resonate together?

It is the result, I think, of a search for some kind of new spirituality—some alternative to what many perceive to be a destructive, manipulative, mechanistic approach to life which, it is said, has raped the earth and robbed humans of their humanity.

To construct this new spirituality, people are drawing on many sources—but not very much on orthodox Christianity, which is viewed as having caused the problems in the first place. The attitude toward Christianity implicit in most of the works and espoused by most of the adherents is perhaps best expressed in the words of the poet Robert Bly. In his introduction to a popular anthology of ecological poetry called *News of the Universe,* he writes,

> The Church at the start of the Christian era didn't know whether to accept the ancient view that we share consciousness with nature or to declare a new era. The Church Fathers were afraid to open the door to too many visions for fear the ancient world would simply flood the Church. As it happened, the Church rejected the Mysteries, smashed the temples, destroyed the relating texts, and lost the doctrines.[1]

The bookstore I am describing represents a large-scale movement to recover those old-world mysteries, that belief in a shared consciousness in nature which, according to Bly and others, the church has suppressed. And let me remind you—this movement generates perhaps the best books on environmental topics. For a kind of religion of the earth is an important part of this eclectic religious movement, sometimes called "new consciousness" or "the New Age." It is most visible on the West Coast, but it is certainly a force throughout the Western world. What do we Christians make of it—especially when it becomes plain that in our attempts to articulate a religiously based attitude toward our use of the earth, we are unavoidably, like it or not, part of the same movement? For like the "New Agers," we are trying to replace the materialist utilitarianism of the past with something new and better.

There are many reasons why it is important for us to know something about the New Age movement. First, it is essential that we recognize the cultural pressures that are affecting our reading of Scripture and the Christian tradition. We are asking relatively new kinds of questions, and we must know as clearly as possible why we are asking them, because it is essential that we recognize both our commonality with and our differences from those who are asking similar questions of Zen Buddhism, Taoism, and native American Indian religion.

There are two further reasons why we should understand

---

1. Bly, *News of the Universe: Poems of Twofold Consciousness* (San Francisco: Sierra Club Books, 1980), p. 9.

the New Age movement. We need to be able to distinguish biblical Christianity from the quasi-pantheistic religion of the earth that crops up frequently in New Age thinking. Recognizing the cultic elements in New Age thought is a good warning against our unwittingly forming yet one more do-it-yourself syncretistic religion. On the other hand, we need to recognize, as many New Age thinkers have, the scope of the scientific and cultural revolution of which the environmental movement is a part—and be able to draw on a diversity of movements, thinkers, and ideas in order to articulate more clearly a Christian position.

In essence, New Age thinking is a complex cluster of ideas that among many groups of people, especially on the West Coast, has the status of a controlling philosophy of life—indeed, a religion. A recent study, for example, polled a sampling of students from Chico State College (in northern California) on their real religious ideas. It showed that the largest group held to the tenets of New Age religion. Christianity was the next most popular belief system. Least appealing was the worldview of scientific materialism.[2] It is usually against this tottering giant that we do our apologetic battles. But the real alternative to Christianity in North America today is not secular materialism; it is rather an eclectic spirituality, loosely based on certain ideas drawn from science, whose diverse adherents regard themselves as prophets of true science, not enemies of it.

Many environmentalists believe that some of the components of New Age thinking provide a better foundation than Christianity upon which to build an ethic for living on the earth. These components can be briefly outlined.

Central to New Age thinking is the conviction that we humans are indeed on the threshold of a "new age," one characterized by a new kind of knowing, which means, most basically, a new kind of science. Here there is considerable dependence on the thinking of Thomas Kuhn, a noted historian and philosopher of science. In his book *The Structure of Scientific Revolutions,* Kuhn claims that science does not—as is popularly thought—progress incrementally, with gradual additions of information to a steadily growing body of knowledge. Instead, he argues, science proceeds through major shifts in its interpretative framework, or paradigm. Explanations in any discipline are made within a particular framework, but over time more and more anomalies ap-

---

2. See Carol Molcar, "Worldview and Purpose in Life" (Master's thesis, University of California at Chico, 1984).

pear that don't seem to fit the framework. If these cannot be resolved, eventually they lead to the abandonment of the old framework in favor of one that more adequately explains the anomalies. Although a new scientific paradigm at first meets with resistance within the established scientific community, it is gradually established (usually championed by younger scientists outside the establishment) and becomes the new framework—one further from error, says Kuhn, but not necessarily closer to truth.[3]

The best examples of such shifts come from physics and astronomy—the most dramatic being the replacement of the Ptolemaic (earth-centered) model of the heavens with the Copernican (sun-centered) model. The Copernican revolution—which really culminated in the seventeenth century with the trial of Galileo—inspired a variety of thinkers and new ideas that ushered in the modern scientific age, a kind of paradigm of paradigms. Central here is the philosophy of René Descartes, a contemporary of Galileo. Descartes argued for the certainty of knowledge, which could be arrived at by a thoughtful mind observing a machine-like universe from a position of lofty detachment. Indeed, certainty, detachment, and the fundamentally mechanistic character of the natural world are all premises that seemed to enter the Western scientific tradition at about this time. A generation later, Newton was able to describe, as it were, the laws by which the mechanism operated, and the brilliant success of his theories provided the framework within which all the sciences operated—or at least to which they aspired—for nearly three hundred years.

It is this Newtonian-Cartesian paradigm of science, interpreted for the public by Francis Bacon's ideas about the necessity of regaining dominion over nature, which New Age thinkers declare is responsible for much of the damage both to the planetary environment and to the human psyche. First astronomy, then physics, chemistry, biology, psychology, sociology, and even philosophy and religion fell under this compelling kind of explanation. According to it (and it so dominates our vision that we have trouble seeing in any other way), the universe is matter

---

3. Kuhn, *The Structure of Scientific Revolutions* (Chicago: University of Chicago Press, 1962). For a good example of the way New Age thinkers have adopted Kuhn's idea of paradigm shift, see Marilyn Ferguson, *The Aquarian Conspiracy: Personal and Social Transformation in the 1980s* (Los Angeles: J. P. Tarcher, 1981), especially chap. 3: "Transformation: Brains Changing, Minds Changing."

in motion, behaving according to laws that we can discover and describe from the viewpoint of a detached observer. First the solar system, then animals, humans, societies, and economies have come to be understood as mechanisms. Thus we have the spectacle of humans trying to manage societies or economies or forests or watersheds as though they were machines amenable to tinkering.[4]

For a variety of reasons, this paradigm proved inadequate to describe the world in which we live. It was adequate up to a point, perhaps, for a limited kind of explanation. But much was not explained. The first flaws in the paradigm were revealed by physics. Investigation into the world of the very small—the subnuclear world—was proceeding in the first decades of this century as though the atom were in fact made of small, discrete particles—as though it were a kind of mechanism. The first contradiction came when Einstein, in developing his theory of relativity, questioned the absolute and unvarying grid of time and space, a fundamental Newtonian presupposition. Time and space are not absolutes, said Einstein, but variables that depend upon the position and the viewpoint of the observer as well as the speed at which the observer is moving. Thus the ideal of a completely detached and objective description of the universe was called into question by the necessity of a viewpoint.

This idea of objective, detached certainty was challenged a little later by Werner Heisenberg in what has come to be known as the indeterminacy principle. He claimed that when we describe the world of the very small, we can be precise about the position of a particle or about its velocity, but we cannot be precise about both. Like Einstein, Heisenberg was pointing out that the perspective from which we ask the questions is not detached; the sort of world we find is dependent on the sort of questions we ask. Again, detachment—and the ideal of a complete, objective description—was called into question.

Even more startling is the picture of the world that has begun to emerge from quantum mechanics. The oddity of that world is shown dramatically in an experiment based on the assertion that certain properties of electrons are not revealed until we choose the kind of question we are going to ask about them. Reference to this experiment—usually referred to as the EPR

---

4. For a good documentation of the consequences of this Newtonian-Cartesian paradigm, see Fritjof Capra, *The Turning Point: Science, Society, and the Rising Culture* (New York: Bantam Books, 1982).

(Einstein-Podolsky-Rosen) experiment—occurs with monotonous regularity in New Age writing. So does reference to "Bell's theorem," an attempt by John S. Bell in 1965 to make some sort of sense of the experiment. Since the experiment does indeed seem to indicate that we live in a dramatically different sort of world than most of us think we live in, it is important to consider it here.[5]

Electrons may be said to "spin" about an axis, but that axis cannot be determined precisely. Fritjof Capra, a noted author reflecting New Age perspectives, explains:

> Whenever a measurement is performed for any axis of rotation, the electron will be found to spin in one or the other direction about that axis. In other words, the particle acquires a definite axis of rotation in the process of measurement, but before the measurement is taken, it cannot generally be said to spin about a definite axis; it merely has a certain tendency, or potentiality, to do so.[6]

The experiment proceeds as follows. We take two particles whose total spin is zero—that is, which are spinning in opposite directions—and separate them. We can separate them any distance—put one on the moon, for example, and one on the earth. Then we determine the direction of spin on one of them. But in effect we determine the direction of spin by the method we choose to discern it. The inexplicable and eerie consequence of the experiment is that no matter how far apart the particles are, they are always spinning in opposite directions. For example, if we determine that the particle on the earth is spinning to the right, then the particle on the moon must be spinning to the left. If we determine, by another method of observation, that the axis of spin requires the particle on the earth to turn to the left, then the particle on the moon must spin to the right.

What the theory requires is that some instantaneous linkage or communication exist between the particles that transmits messages faster than the speed of light. The problem comes from considering the system as though it were a two-part system instead of a single system. Niels Bohr, the scientist who developed the modern theory of atomic structure, noted this paradox, and Capra paraphrases him: "The two-particle system is an indivisi-

---

5. Meditations on the significance of the EPR experiment abound. A good straightforward summary is provided by Edward S. Fry, "The Einstein-Podolsky-Rosen Experiment: Past, Present, and Future" (Paper delivered at Texas A & M University).

6. Capra, *The Turning Point*, p. 84.

ble whole, even if the particles are separated by a great distance; the system cannot be analyzed in terms of independent parts."[7]

If this oddity—which is apparently inescapable—is in fact true, then the universe is fundamentally different from the mechanistic model assumed by the physics and (in general) the science of the last three hundred years. The premise of that science is that we can analyze the parts of a mechanistic system in detachment from them and from the system. The troubling—and in some sense exhilarating—effect of modern physics is the recognition that we cannot (as in the Cartesian model) loftily separate ourselves from what we are investigating, nor can the "parts" of the universe be neatly separated from each other.

These findings and theories have been around for half a century, but they are just beginning to filter down and out from the towers of theoretical physics. Christians have not done much with them, perhaps because we also have been too comfortable with the categories of a mechanistic world. But a generation of post-Christian seekers has fastened on these phenomena as proof of the bankruptcy of a spirit-less materialism. Books like Capra's *The Tao of Physics* and Gary Zukav's *The Dancing Wu Li Masters* have drawn all sorts of correlations between physics and what Aldous Huxley called "the perennial philosophy."[8] The term refers to a kind of monism found frequently in Oriental religion: the belief that all is one, that my mind in some sense determines reality, and that the world is ultimately an illusion based on my perception of it.

In his book *The Turning Point*, Capra sums up the philosophical and religious implications of quantum theory:

> Quantum theory has shown that subatomic particles are not isolated grains of matter but are probability patterns, interconnections in an inseparable cosmic web that includes the human observer and her consciousness. Relativity theory has made the cosmic web come alive, so to speak, by revealing its essentially dynamic character; by showing that its activity is the very essence of its being. In modern physics, the image of the universe as a machine has been transcended by a view of it as one indivisible, dynamic whole whose parts are essentially interrelated and can be understood only as patterns of a cosmic process. At the subatomic level the interrelations and interactions between the parts of the

---

7. Capra, *The Turning Point*, p. 85.

8. Huxley makes his case in *The Perennial Philosophy* (New York: Harper, 1944).

whole are more fundamental than the parts themselves. There is motion but there are, ultimately, no moving objects; there is activity but there are no actors; there are no dancers, there is only the dance.[9]

The troubling implication of the EPR experiment—that two things (and potentially all things, the whole universe) can be related "non-locally," and hence understood as participants in some vast order that transcends our perception of the parts as separate— has been taken up in an intriguing way by physicist David Bohm. He argues for "the unbroken wholeness of the totality of existence as an undivided flowing movement without borders."[10]

Bohm uses a precise mechanical analogy to suggest the kind of relationship that the EPR experiment hints at. Consider a cylinder of highly viscous fluid in which is suspended a droplet of ink that is insoluble in the medium. If the fluid is stirred in a single direction with a mechanical device, the droplet will be drawn out in finer and finer threads until it is invisible. If, however, the stirring movement is exactly reversed, the invisible threads of ink will return to their original form, and the original droplet will suddenly reappear. This shows that the ink has been enfolded in its fluid medium and is everywhere present throughout it. Such an experiment seems to illustrate the nature of reality as revealed by modern physics. Bohm describes that order when he sums up his argument in *Wholeness and the Implicate Order*:

> We proposed that a new notion of order is involved here, which we called the *implicate order* (from a Latin root meaning "to enfold" or "to fold inward"). In terms of the implicate order one may say that everything is enfolded into everything. This contrasts with the *explicate order* now dominant in physics in which things are *unfolded* in the sense that each thing lies only in its own particular region of space (and time) and outside the regions belonging to other things.[11]

The idea that "everything is enfolded" in everything else is a powerful one, and it strikes resonant chords in many disciplines. One of those disciplines, of course, is ecology. Though the "enfolding" concept is a bit more radical, Bohm's idea sounds very similar to Barry Commoner's assertion in *The Closing Circle* that

---

9. Capra, *The Turning Point*, pp. 91-92.
10. Bohm, *Wholeness and the Implicate Order* (London: Routledge & Kegan Paul, 1980), p. 172.
11. Bohm, *Wholeness and the Implicate Order*, p. 177.

"everything is connected to everything else," and to the oft-quoted statement by John Muir that "when you try to pick out anything by itself, you find it hitched to the universe." The hint of universal mutual involvement is also quite close to the ideal (or nightmare) of the "global village" promised by modern communications, in which each person is (at least potentially) in contact with every other person on the globe.

The concept of the implicate order and the vision of an integrated universe which underlies it can well be illuminated by a Christian understanding. Christians, however, have not thought much about the theological implications of modern physics.

But the religious dimension of these ideas has been picked up enthusiastically by many in the so-called New Age movement. In addition to the resonances I have mentioned, more abstruse ones have been noted that make explicit their religious character. For example, both Capra and Marilyn Ferguson, author of *The Aquarian Conspiracy*, quote this Hindu Sutra: "In the heaven of Indra there is said to be a network of pearls so arranged that if you look at one you see all the others reflected in it. In the same way, each object in the world is not merely itself but involves every other object, and in fact *is* in every other object."[12] Many have gone further, seeing in this apparent indication of universal interrelationship a confirmation of the prevalent Hindu and Buddhist view that fundamentally the world is *Maya*, illusion: we create it by dreaming of it, by our perception of it, much as we determine the "spin" on a particle by our means of investigating it.

But one of the most intriguing things that is being done with the idea of implicate order is the analogy being drawn between Bohm's "enfolding" and the nature of knowledge encoded in the brain. Here the key figure is neuroscientist Karl Pribram. At one time Pribram worked with Karl Lashley, famous for his (ultimately futile) attempt to try to locate the physical site of a particular memory in the brain. In experiments with laboratory animals Pribram discovered that physical eradication of parts of the brain simply does not eliminate storage of a memory—rather, the memory seems in some mysterious way to be nonlocalized. Pribram's contribution to the discussion is his use of the concept of the hologram to understand the brain's functioning.

Here we must detour briefly into a curious feature of that

---

12. Cited in Ferguson, *The Aquarian Conspiracy*, p. 185.

increasingly frequent technological oddity, the holographic image. A hologram is the image of an object made from the interference pattern of light waves from two sources reflected off that object. When this image is viewed by the coherent light of the laser, it apears three-dimensional. But the intriguing thing is not so much the 3-D character of the resulting image but the fact that *the whole image is contained in any one part of it.* If a piece of the hologram is broken away, the remaining portion will reconstruct the complete image. Pribram likened the brain's information storage system to the hologram, and many believe that it is also analogous to Bohm's implicate order of the universe.

Pribram went on to ask the difficult question, If the brain is a hologram, who is seeing the image? Is there indeed "a ghost in the machine"? Or is the case rather—as Pribram assumed and as writers like Marilyn Ferguson are quick to agree—that there is no "who" nor "I" but only a participant in the dance? To some, this idea opens the door to the supernatural—or, as it has become fashionable to call it, "the transcendent." Ferguson puts it this way:

> In this framework, psychic phenomena are only by-products of the simultaneous-everywhere matrix. Individual brains are bits of the greater hologram. They have access under certain circumstances to all the information in the total cybernetic system. Synchronicity—the web of coincidence that seems to have some higher purpose or connectedness—also fits in with the holographic model. . . . Psychokinesis, mind affecting matter, may be a natural result of interaction at the primary level.[13]

Thus a foundation is laid for asserting the legitimacy of a variety of occult and paranormal experiences.

The holographic model of consciousness is just one of the ideas from current research into the nature of the brain that have been assimilated into the loose religious synthesis of the new consciousness.[14] Another concept even more popular in modern pop-science is the increasingly well-substantiated difference in function between the left and the right hemispheres of the brain. The phrases "right brain" and "left brain" have become clichés. As everyone "knows" by now, the left hemisphere of the brain controls linear thought and language; the right hemisphere is

---

13. Ferguson, *The Aquarian Conspiracy*, p. 182.

14. For a good summary of the metaphysical speculation stirred up by holography, see *The Holographic Paradigm and Other Paradoxes: Exploring the Leading Edge of Science*, ed. Ken Wilber (Boulder, Colo.: Shambhala Press, 1982).

more intuitive, less analytical, and seems adept at grasping gestalt relationships and whole patterns.[15]

In general, our society has increasingly stressed the importance of left-brain functions. When music and art are taught, for example, they are likely to be taught in terms of verbal principles (the sort of knowledge which can be tested with a multiple-choice examination). Post-Cartesian science—logical analysis by a detached mind deliberating on a world separate from itself that it can reduce to discrete entities—is clearly (in this model) a "left-brain" sort of science. Likewise, the argument goes, our approach to success, to human relationships, and to nature itself have all been excessively analytical; the nonverbal, holistic aspects of those relationships—the sort that are grasped by the right-brain functions—are not likely to be emphasized.

A good example is our approach to medicine, which increasingly has dealt with smaller and smaller subsystems of the body (witness the proliferation of specialists) and not with the overall, intuitively grasped concept and experience of *health.* Thus "holistic health" (stressing diet, exercise, environment, and various spiritual connections) is one of the most influential aspects of New Age thinking.

The revolution in physics—which has long held a kind of privileged status as the zenith of science, the supreme left-brain activity—has been disturbing because it suggests a world whose nature can best be understood not by linear thought, a left-brain activity, but by intuitive grasping, a right-brain activity. Quantum mechanics, the EPR experiment, Bohm's reflections on the implicate order, Pribram's holistic model for consciousness—all of these seem to suggest the necessity of a greater involvement of the intuitive right hemisphere of the brain, which is more likely to grasp things as whole rather than as parts.

Since science is associated with the Christian West and with ideas of man as dominant over nature, made in the image of a God who is likewise dominant and transcendent, the popular New Age movement usually discards this Christian religious paradigm in favor of the religions of the East, which affirm a God or gods (if any) who are only part of the process, and which allow one to say in effect, "I am God; I am the universe." Those who hold such a position do not trouble with analysis, but are con-

---

15. A good popular summary of the findings of "split-brain" research is Thomas Blakeslee, *The Right Brain: A New Understanding of the Unconscious Mind and Its Creative Powers* (New York: Berkley Books, 1980).

cerned with grasping the whole. Thus the environmentalist movement, which stresses the unity of the earth and our oneness with it, is far more likely to have among its adherents members of New Age sensibility than Christians. Accordingly, Christians who try to develop an environmentalist ethic in such a framework run the serious danger of simply parroting New Age ideas.

There is one more aspect of the New Age movement that I want to touch on before treating Christian responses to it: the so-called human potentials movement. Like much in New Age thinking, this is really too broad and diffuse to be called a movement. The label applies to a wide variety of techniques, therapies, and disciplines that are intended to put people in touch with their own feelings, their own potential. Often this enabling is understood as an attempt to put to rest the analytical chatter of left-brain functions in order to awaken depths of right-brain-controlled creativity.

Like the New Age movement, the human potentials movement is in many ways a reaction against a description of human nature in terms of the very mechanistic science that seems to be so severely threatened by the findings of modern physics. First Freudianism and then behaviorism made humans into things. The human potentials movement, while not necessarily denying the reductive descriptions of these two schools of psychology, asserts that we have depths and potentials that no mere animal, no mere thing, can ever have.

The movement draws from a variety of humanist psychotherapies,[16] but most are traceable to the thought of Abraham Maslow, who defined a hierarchy of human needs that went beyond the merely animal to culminate in the need for self-actualization. And the ultimate in self-actualization is (paradoxically) transcendence, the ability of a person to reach beyond himself and become one with all of reality. This definition of transcendence as the highest human need is often evoked in definitions of psychedelic and sexual experience as well as in a variety of experiences of nature. "Self-transcendence," for example, is often an important element in modern arguments for the importance of wilderness, which focus not so much on stewardship of and responsibility for the land as on the capability of the properly trained and equipped individual to "discover himself" in rock-

---

16. A good summary of the currents of psychological thought feeding into the "human potentials" stream is Francis Adeney, "The Flowering of the Human Potentials Movement," *Spiritual Counterfeits Project Journal* 5 (Winter 1981-82): 7-18.

climbing, white-water rafting, backpacking, and so forth (the kind of experience promoted by programs like Outward Bound).

Many of these activities and attitudes that lead to fulfilled human potential are right-brain activities, suggesting that the left hemisphere of the brain is a master that has enslaved and repressed the intuitive—thus the fascination with techniques for disengaging linear thought, drawn especially from Zen, Yoga, Indian vision quests, and even Christian mysticism. It is instructive to note here how the same movement has surfaced—with a great deal of vitality—in the church, in the form of charismatic movements, healing, greater emphasis on worship and the sacraments, and a rediscovery of the "spiritual" (some would say "mystical") traditions of Christianity. And it is natural that nourishment for increasing human potential is drawn from the holistic insights of ecology and from the implicate order of the new physics.

Certainly the aspect of the human potentials movement with the greatest impact—and perhaps the greatest validity—is feminism. The attempt to regain and clearly state a feminine perspective on the world plays a large part in the New Age movement, and a feminist reading of human attitudes toward nature forms an increasingly significant—and compelling—voice on environmental issues generally.[17]

Let me briefly summarize these feminist arguments, some of which have already become an unavoidable part of our cultural baggage. Western science, the "old paradigm" which I have sketched, was shaped in a patriarchal society that had little place for women's contributions. Thus (though many feminists are extremely uncomfortable in talking about fundamental differences between men and women in thought and attitude, lest that lead to a new justification for male domination), this science is informed by the "masculine" penchant for self-assertion and domination, not by the more "feminine" tendencies toward nurturing and intuition.[18]

This masculine, assertive way of knowing quickly replaces language that reverentially describes nature in feminine terms—

17. See especially Carolyn Merchant, *Death in Nature: Women, Ecology, and the Scientific Revolution* (San Francisco: Harper & Row, 1980).

18. Note that there seems to be a loose correlation between "feminine" and "right-brain" characteristics on the one hand, and "masculine" and "left-brain" characteristics on the other. Such a correlation is often assumed, but it hasn't been established in any conclusive way.

as though it were a mother or wife (consider not only the common term "Mother Nature" but also that profound synonym for farmer, "husbandman")—with language that describes nature simply as neutral, dead matter. This largely masculine approach to knowledge proceeds, as we have seen, by means of dissection and analysis. It places little emphasis on synthesis, wholeness, or nurturing. The premise of detachment, so much a part of the Cartesian approach to things, is a favorite masculine posture, whereas women have often been accused of being too involved with their feelings (via, it is said, an attachment to their bodies that makes detachment less possible—"biology is destiny") to adequately investigate or manage the world of nature.

In her history of science entitled *Death in Nature: Women, Ecology, and the Scientific Revolution,* Carolyn Merchant argues that it is no coincidence that the period of greatest persecution of women as witches was also the period marked by the early successes of the scientific revolution—that is, the early seventeenth century. Merchant makes a convincing case that much of the language of Bacon's *Novum Organum,* his development of the inductive method, is drawn from the language of witch trials. In essence he said that we must put nature to the test to know and control her, just as we must put women to the test because of their uncanny and possibly sacred kinds of insights.[19]

Today, with many reasons apparent for questioning the adequacy of our old "masculine" ways of knowing nature, we find an argument for a more nurturing kind of knowledge that might be led by women or by the "feminine" side of men (for an important part of the New Age theory—following Jung—is that we are psychically androgynous). This idea is dramatized in Ernest Callenbach's *Ecotopia,* a book that creates an environmentalist's Utopia. In this hypothetical nation (consisting of northern California, Oregon, and Washington, which have seceded from the union in order to form an environmentally wise society), the leader is a woman. Women also hold prominent places in such important activities as forestry, which is seriously, almost religiously managed on a sustained-yield basis, with much reverence accorded to the spirits of the trees. Along with this call for more feminine involvement in science, management, and resource decisions come some compelling reasons to recover the old idea of nature, the earth, as a nurturing mother. In part this is

19. Merchant, *Death in Nature*, pp. 164ff.

a kind of mythologizing of the findings of ecology, which show how we are indeed nurtured by the ecosphere.

Even more basic and radical imagery of the earth as a living creature comes from James Lovelock and Barbara Margulis, who argue, on the basis of atmospheric chemistry, that the earth is itself an organism, perhaps the largest organism, and that it has maintained, over geological eons of time, an atmosphere conducive to life.[20] Lovelock contends that "the entire range of living matter on Earth, from whales to viruses and from oaks to algae, could be regarded as constituting a single living entity, capable of manipulating the Earth's atmosphere to suit its overall needs and endowed with faculties and powers far beyond those of its constituent parts."[21]

The name for this planet-sized creature is Gaia, a Greek name for the goddess of the earth—and increasing references to the earth as Gaia, a kind of feminine, planetary organism, occur in New Age literature and art. For example, an enormously popular piece of music is Paul Winter's *Missa Gaia*, a "mass of the earth" first performed with animal sounds in the Cathedral of St. John the Divine in New York. But the question of who or what is being worshiped—the earth or the creator of that earth—is not well-defined in this moving piece of music. Winter describes performing the piece in the cathedral as "awakening a sense of the sacred"—and defines the sacred as a sense of "connectedness with the universe."[22] The universe, not God. And of course the most important part of that connection is recognizing our connectedness to Gaia, earth, the great mother.

What is the relevance of all of this for a Christian environmental ethic? Let me begin by summing up the aspects of New Age thinking I have touched on in order to try to show the underlying unity of the movement. Its firmest foundation, I have suggested, is its rethinking of a model of science. In place of the detached kind of science and the mechanistic view of nature, we find emerging a picture—first sketched by modern physics and later augmented by ecological biology—of a much different kind of knowing. In this "new paradigm" the knower is inseparable from what is being known. What is known is not a mechanism of

20. See Lovelock, *Gaia: A New Look at Life on Earth* (New York: Oxford University Press, 1979).

21. Lovelock, cited in the liner notes of *Missa Gaia: Earth Mass* by Paul Winter (Living Music Records, 1982).

22. Winter, liner notes of *Missa Gaia*.

individual parts but a great interrelated order—David Bohm's implicate order, or, in more mystical terms, "the great dance."

Not only is the nature of the world that we know being questioned; so also is the nature of our knowledge. Our brains seem to store knowledge in a way at least analogous to the enfolded, holographic world. And we are coming to discover that there is much more to our knowing than analyzing the pieces: there is also a creative, intuitive, whole-knowing part of our brains that our culture has long suppressed.

In reaction to the dehumanizing tendencies of the prevailing definition of knowledge—with its dehumanizing definitions of the human—has come a host of movements, techniques, and therapies that promise self-fulfillment, even self-transcendence. Among the greatest of these is feminism's defense of a nurturing, holistic kind of knowing that is seen as being better for both people and the planet than the masculine, analytic, self-assertive knowing that has (it is argued) brought us to the brink of nuclear war, environmental catastrophe, or both. We have only to take our future into our hands and fulfill our potential as the sentient members of the planet, the "handymen for the earth," as Lewis Thomas puts it.[23] And since Western Christianity is inextricably tied up with ideas of patriarchalism, hierarchy, detachment, and dominion, it is more likely that we will find the spiritual resources we need elsewhere—thus the interest in neolithic religions and religions of the East, which affirm the unity of all things.

Overall, the goals of this New Age approach are stated most clearly in the statement of belief of Lindisfarne, a sort of New Age think tank that includes people like scientist James Lovelock, astronaut Rusty Schweikert, and poet Gary Snyder. They describe themselves as follows:

> Lindisfarne is an association of individuals and groups around the world devoted to the study and realization of a new planetary culture. Seeking for the sacred in all forms of human activity and culture, members of the Association share the following goals: the spiritual transformation of individual consciousness; the realization of the inner harmony of the great universal religions; the resacralization of the relations between nature and culture through the development of an appropriate technology for a meta-

---

23. Thomas, *The Lives of a Cell: Notes of a Biology Watcher* (New York: Viking Press, 1974), p. 106. Thomas's remarkable essays, in this volume and in *The Medusa and the Snail: More Notes of a Biology Watcher* (New York: Viking Press, 1979), are perhaps the most eloquent argument for the earth as organism.

industrial culture; and the illumination of the spiritual dimensions of world order.[24]

What is a suitable Christian response to all of this? Some Christians have seen only the religious aspects of the new consciousness movement, and have sounded an alarm. They warn of Satanism, witchcraft, the Antichrist, and even a worldwide conspiracy behind all who advocate, for example, the necessity of developing a planetary awareness, or working toward the redistribution of the earth's wealth. This reaction is most clearly represented in a book published in 1983 that is read like a Bible in some Christian circles: *The Hidden Dangers of the Rainbow: The New Age Movement and Our Coming Age of Barbarism* by Constance Cumbey. Cumbey views some of the more far-out members of the movement, such as David Spangler of the Findhorn community, as the direct descendants of various theosophical and occult movements that she traces back into the nineteenth century. Discounting the substantial science behind the ecological, physical, and physiological components of the movement, she says the real goal is power: world power wielded by a small elite, which understands itself quite consciously as anti-Christian.[25] Her arguments are echoed and amplified in a more recent book by Dave Hunt called *Peace, Prosperity and the Coming Holocaust: The New Age Movement in Prophecy.* Like Cumbey, Hunt argues that the New Age rhetoric about a more just world order, a sense of planetary responsibility, and a redistribution of resources is only a disguise for satanic tyranny.[26]

Although these books involve a fair amount of conspiracy-hunting (that time-honored element of American fundamentalism) and large doses of extreme dispensational prophecy-reading of the kind found in Hal Lindsey's books, it would be a mistake for Christians to completely discount the concerns of these writers. No Christian can affirm, with David Spangler, that we are each our own Christ. And there is a frightening element in the New Age attempts to bring together occult and scientific knowledge. One is reminded of C. S. Lewis's *Screwtape Letters* and Screwtape's fervent belief that one of the solidest achievements of Hell would be the creation of a "materialist magician," one who

---

24. Cited in the liner notes of *Missa Gaia*.

25. Cumbey, *The Hidden Dangers of the Rainbow: The New Age Movement and Our Coming Age of Barbarism* (Shreveport, La.: Huntington House, 1983).

26. Hunt, *Peace, Prosperity and the Coming Holocaust* (Eugene, Oreg.: Harvest House, 1983).

uncritically accepted the findings of science but who also operated out of a sincere belief in spiritual forces, which are likely to be Satan in disguise.[27] These works critical of the New Age movement are at least trying to perform a valuable service for the Christian community by pointing out the anti-Christian forces that we sometimes ally ourselves with uncritically.

Nevertheless, such works are unfortunate because they greatly exaggerate the occult element in the New Age movement and ignore the genuine challenges to established thinking represented by breakthroughs in physics, biology, and brain research. Perhaps even more distressing, writers like Hunt and Cumbey dismiss any attempt at environmental stewardship—even any use of terms like "ecological" and "holistic"—as part of the plot.

Cumbey is particularly distressed by Christians who suggest we need to develop a global consciousness or that we have an obligation to work for the redistribution of wealth in the world. She finds New Age thinking infesting many Christian writers and organizations. For example, she insists that Tom Sine's *Mustard Seed Conspiracy* is riddled with New Age ideas: that he uses the term itself approximately 150 times, and that he quotes with approval such notorious New Age thinkers as Jeremy Rifkin, Hazel Henderson, Buckminster Fuller, Robert Heilbroner, and Richard Barnet. Cumbey also accuses Sine of "quoting with approval" excerpts from the "horrendous Global 2000 report," as well as Willy Brandt's North-South summit report. But worse than all of these "guilts by association," Cumbey maintains, is Sine's calling for a new way of life among Christians, a way that will result in a different distribution of wealth.

Cumbey is equally hard on Ron Sider. She criticizes him first because *Rich Christians in an Age of Hunger* is co-published by two organizations that she believes to be "defiled": InterVarsity Press, which she claims is tainted by New Age ideas, and Paulist Press, "whose books," she says, "tend more towards socialism and outright New Age thinking than they do towards orthodox

---

27. Says Screwtape: "I have great hopes that we [the devils] shall learn in due time how to emotionalize and mythologize their science to such an extent that what is, in effect, a belief in us (though not under that name) will creep in while the human mind remains closed to belief in the Enemy. The 'Life Force,' the worship of sex, and some aspects of Psychoanalysis may here prove useful. If once we can produce our perfect work—the Materialist Magician, the man not using, but veritably worshipping, what he vaguely calls 'Forces' while denying the existence of 'spirits'— then the end of the war will be in sight" (C. S. Lewis, *The Screwtape Letters* [New York: Harcourt, Brace & World, 1961], pp. 39-40).

Christian thinking." Cumbey continues, "The first thing noticeable about Sider's book to one versed in New Age lore is his use of a vocabulary prevalent among New Agers. Words such as Spaceship Earth, vanguard, holistic, New Age, and global village, are a common part of his vocabulary."[28] She goes on to point out that Sider's thoughts on the Old Testament Jubilee are sinisterly similar to plans to inaugurate the Age of Aquarius by a freezing and redistribution of wealth.

Another of Cumbey's wolves in sheep's clothing is *Earthkeeping*, the book that came out of a study several of us did a few years ago at Calvin College.[29] Cumbey says that in our book, "the New Age political program is laid out in its entirety—including a *duty* for Christians to support globalization of our structures." She takes particular exception to our argument that redemption involves not lifting humanity out of nature but redeeming nature with and through man. "If I read my Bible correctly," she says, "our peace was to be with God—not nature. The Calvin College position distinctly smacks of both Monism ([the] concept that God created the earth and then diffused himself equally throughout the universe) and animism. God was going to make all things new—not redeem nature along with man."[30] Cumbey continues in this vein. In response to our pointing out that Eastern Orthodoxy has stressed that line of interpretation which says that nature is to be redeemed along with man, Cumbey says that this turning to the East is the sort of thing one would expect of New Agers, who enthusiastically embrace Eastern religions.

It would be an easy matter to discount or refute Cumbey's argument, which is an odd mixture of innuendoes, half-truths, and guilt by association. I don't think that kind of refutation is necessary. But a few observations do need to be made about Cumbey's work. For one thing, it has struck a responsive chord in a large number of Christians. Because of the work of Cumbey and others who see the New Age movement as wholly satanic, many Christians, were they to read what has been written on Christian environmental concern, would not see this material as articulating an aspect of the Gospel. Rather, they would see it as a dangerous, anti-Christian conspiracy in which we have become entangled through a kind of nature-loving tender-mindedness.

---

28. Cumbey, *The Hidden Dangers of the Rainbow*, pp. 156-57.
29. See *Earthkeeping: Christian Stewardship of Natural Resources*, ed. Loren Wilkinson (Grand Rapids: Eerdmans, 1980).
30. Cumbey, *The Hidden Dangers of the Rainbow*, pp. 162-63.

We can attribute the popularity of such responses in part to fundamentalism's fruitless affair with predictive prophecy and its penchant for finding heresies and conspiracies. But I think the popularity goes deeper than that. The fact is, absurd as Cumbey's arguments are, they contain a grain of truth that many Christians are responding to. There *is*, as I have tried to outline, a major shift in consciousness, values, and epistemology occurring in our time. It does not smack of the conspiracy that Cumbey detects, but it nevertheless exists as a powerful alternative to Christian faith. And there is no question that it is, or points to, a number of "spiritual counterfeits." In other words, though Cumbey's and Hunt's warnings are almost entirely wrongheaded, we do indeed need to be warned. For, as I argued at the beginning, in most cases we have been led to environmental concern not because of the unavoidable conclusions of Scripture but because of an almost unavoidable, irresistible cultural pressure.

Today's Christians have done nothing new in casting the Gospel in terms of their own culture—indeed, it is essential to the nature of the Gospel. The very specificity of the Incarnation and the human nature of revelation testify to God's willingness to let the eternal message be expressed in local, temporal, limited terms. It is likewise true that as time has unfolded, the content of the Gospel has unfolded. If we now see implications in Genesis, in the Psalms, in the Gospels, and in Paul's Christological passages that are relevant to a theology of "earthkeeping," that is not to say that the Gospel changes, but that it unfolds new dimensions over time.

This has been true from the beginning. New cultural questions in the fourth century led to the Christological formulations of Nicea. In the Eastern church, the conflict with iconoclastic Islam in the eighth and ninth centuries led to the development of a defense of imagery and art. In the sixteenth century the excesses of the Roman Catholic Church brought about a great clarification, a new understanding, of the nature of salvation by grace.

Thus a major reason for being aware of the constellation of ideas foundational to the New Age movement is hermeneutic— that is, it has to do with the way we approach and interpret the book that is the basis of our conclusions, the Bible. If we are to avoid the criticism that we make the Bible simply a mirror of our own concerns and preoccupations, it is exceedingly important that we recognize clearly why theologians today are finding things in Scripture that Christians never noticed before. I do not mean to imply that these are not valid findings. Christian theology is a record of the dialogue between Scripture, which does not change, and history, which does. It does not compromise the authority and inspiration of Scripture to recognize that when we come to the Bible with new questions, we may find in it new answers—a process that causes us to reflect not only on the nature of interpretation and of knowledge itself, but also on Christian teaching about the illuminating and comforting Spirit of God, which, Jesus promises, will guide the church into all truth. Nevertheless, clarity and honesty alike demand that we acknowledge the cultural framework of this current requestioning—which in many ways is a reinterpretation—of Scripture.

We Christian environmentalists have perhaps come dangerously close to making biblical Christianity a kind of worship of the earth. In our affirmations of humans as creatures embedded in the web of life, we might have come close to forgetting that we are also creatures made in God's image. In arguing from Scripture for the immanence of God, we dare not forget God's transcendence. In discovering that the Bible communicates in story, song, and parable to the right hemisphere of the brain, we cannot forget that the Bible also communicates in precept, rule, and logic to the left hemisphere of the brain.

In short, we need to be careful. Scripture and the Christian tradition contain rich resources for the shaping of a deeper, more biblical view of creation and our relationship to it. We are finally beginning to understand the scope of what Paul meant when he declared that "If any one is in Christ, he is [not only "a new creature," as our older translations have it, but] *a new creation*" (italics mine). But we need to make such judgments cautiously, carefully, recognizing that we cannot simply make Scripture say what we want it to say. We cannot simply pick and choose from the smorgasbord of Christian tradition; we must be guided by good exegesis, good hermeneutics, good history—and by the Holy Spirit.

But we need to be guided as well by good sense, which makes us open to understand the creation in which we are placed. This creation seems stranger and stranger to us every day, as our science shows us more and more strange things about our planet, about the nature of matter, and about the nature of the mind with which we are asked to love and serve our Maker. It is tragic for the church, for the cause of Christ, that in response to such findings as I have described, many thoughtful people find it necessary to turn to Taoism, to Zen, to Hindu thought, to animism, to magic. If we as Christians can understand our world, and God's world, more rightly, perhaps these people—upon confronting the strangeness of creation, its unity, the necessary personality of all knowing and being known—can turn instead to the great "implicate order" of him in whom all things consist, without whom nothing was made: the Lamb slain before the foundation of the world, and for the life of the world.

Invitation to Wonder: Toward a Theology of Nature

ROBERT P. MEYE

O LORD, our Lord
how majestic is thy name in all the earth!

Thou whose glory above the heavens is chanted
  by the mouth of babes and infants,
thou hast founded a bulwark because of thy foes,
  to still the enemy and the avenger.

When I look at thy heavens, the work of thy fingers,
  the moon and the stars which thou hast established;
what is man that thou art mindful of him,
  and the son of man that thou dost care for him?

Yet thou hast made him little less than God,
  and dost crown him with glory and honor.
Thou has given him dominion over the works of thy hands;
  thou hast put all things under his feet,
all sheep and oxen,
  and also the beasts of the field,
the birds of the air, and the fish of the sea,
  whatever passes along the paths of the sea.

O LORD, our Lord,
  how majestic is thy name in all the earth!

PSALM 8

ROBERT P. MEYE, Dean of the School of Theology of Fuller Theological Seminary, has served in that capacity since 1977. He also serves as Professor of New Testament Interpretation in that school. He came to Fuller from Northern Baptist Theological Seminary, where he served as a faculty member from 1962-1977 and as dean from 1971-1977. A magna cum laude graduate of the University of Basel, Meye studied under such luminaries as Karl Barth, Oscar Cullmann, Walther Eichrodt, and Bo Reicke at Basel, as well as Eduard Schweizer at Zurich.

INTRODUCTION

The Invitation to Wonder

Several millennia ago, the Psalmist, beholding creation, was invited to wonder. Today, we who are devoted to the task of developing a theology of nature can only emulate the Psalmist. To contemplate nature is an invitation to wonder, and that in several senses. We are called to wonder in the basic, religious sense. We stand in awe of a "power" greater than ourselves as we contemplate the infinite space and the teeming complexity of life that surrounds us and has surrounded humankind from "the beginning." So overwhelming is the invitation to wonder that one wonders (in another sense of the word) if we are really capable of penetrating to a worthy theology of nature. We "wonder" whether we have the resources, the patience, and the receptive hearts and minds required to penetrate and to understand adequately the world of nature about us.

We are also invited to wonder by our more recent religious heritage. The church itself, where Christian life has been nurtured and has been taught the deep things of the faith, too seldom ventures into the Old Testament, where the more extensive witness to God the Creator is stored up. For a variety of reasons, it remains largely a closed book to most Christians. It is perhaps this closure that has generated a second problem: When the church has appealed to the Old Testament, specifically with respect to the creation of nature, it has repeatedly locked horns with contemporary science. So much so, in fact, that the careful study of the creation material and other related biblical passages remains largely the domain of a few dedicated scholars. To be sure, the biblical materials do not answer all our questions. And interpretations of the creation narratives and other biblical material are often a battleground of theological endeavor, if not a wilderness in which theological students wander with no certain destination. Yes, the place of nature in the biblical materials is indeed an invitation to wonder.

But nature in the biblical materials elicits wonder, first and foremost, as the attitude accompanying the praise and thanksgiving of the Triune Creator God. There is no facet of revelation, short of the Incarnation, that offers more cause for wonder than

Unless otherwise noted, the biblical citations in this essay are taken from the Revised Standard Version of the Bible, copyrighted 1946, 1952, © 1971, 1973.

the revelation of creation displayed in the creation narratives and related passages. Psalm 8 stands as an enduring road marker on the pilgrimage of faith, a lasting reminder that the world of nature about us has always been an invitation to wonder for the faithful. But faith seeks understanding. That is our task, and that is the task of a theology of nature.

Coming to Terms with Terms

The task before us requires clarity, at least as much clarity as is available. Therefore, a word is in order concerning the phrase "theology of nature." In a real sense, every word in the phrase needs at least some explication.

The term "theology" is a reminder that our approach to what we provisionally call "nature" begins from a special vantage point. We may be layperson or scientist; we may possess more empirical data regarding a given facet of the heavens or the earth than any other living being. Nonetheless, to say "theology" is to recognize that we bring a very special outfitting to our task. Theology stands for a privileged—but therefore all the more responsible—position. It is the position of those who know that God has spoken regarding nature, and that we thus have available to us a repository of his speaking in Holy Scripture. Those who are humble before God's voice will recognize the limitations that God has placed upon his speaking and upon our understanding, so that the "theologian" will be the first to confess "wonder" still at the "mystery" of nature.[1] The theologian, with the Word of God in hand and mind and heart, looks at the world from a privileged position—but the theologian is also obliged to look at the world with the eyes and from the position of a scientist. Indeed, a Christian theologian lives in the faith that God has revealed himself in nature, and will give the more diligence to hearing the word "writ large in nature," but this against the horizon of the Word spoken even more surely through prophets, and finally through Jesus Christ, the Son.

"Nature"—what do we mean by this word? There are a variety of ways in which we typically define nature, but for our purposes we can use a simple definition. By "nature" we mean first of all that about us which is not primarily the product of human activity; this includes the heavens and the earth, with the

---

1. See chap. 6 in Karl Barth, *Evangelical Thought: An Introduction*, trans. Grover Foley (Grand Rapids: Eerdmans, 1963).

mighty oceans, fish and fowl, reptiles—all things living, and all things that provide the supporting envelope for and context of life. Christian faith understands and believes that all this is the handiwork of God. However, because God has placed human-kind in the world, to live and multiply and work, the face of nature has been altered through the "natural" activity of the race.

Ordinarily, theologians prefer to use the language of "creation": God is the "Creator" who "creates" the "creatures" who dwell in the splendor of "creation." This language draws constant attention to the dependency of the creature and the creation upon the Creator. The problem with the word "nature" is that all too often it is treated as a proper noun—that is, "Nature" is accorded a personified dignity and status independent of any outside agency, personal or otherwise,[2] above all the One whom Christians worship as God the Creator. When this happens, all sorts of "powers" are turned loose in the human spirit. It is an anomaly that the worship of God's *good* creation has evoked some of the basest responses in the human spirit.

Finally, a passing word regarding the modest preposition "of." When we say that something is "of" something else, we are usually designating belonging or origin. (There are, of course, a variety of other meanings, but the two mentioned tend to predominate.) If only because of these meanings, we must be careful (calling upon our earlier comments concerning theology/revelation) to remember always that we are concerned not with a theology *induced from* nature, but with a theology *brought to* the observation of nature, as a fruit of divine revelation. Thus it is our concern here to approach nature, the created order, from the perspective of God, who gifts us with wisdom from above so that we can understand him, our world, and ourselves in a way that makes us wise unto salvation. What, then, are the parameters of such a "theology of nature," a theology rooted in belief in God the Creator?

THE PARAMETERS OF A THEOLOGY OF NATURE
God the Creator

The canon appropriately begins with the revelation of God as the Creator, the One who gives being, form, and substance to all that

---

2. See George S. Hendry, *Theology of Nature* (Philadelphia: Westminster Press, 1980), pp. 54-74.

is (Gen. 1-3). This revelation is the *constant* basis of biblical faith: throughout the canon, God is worshiped as the Creator. Whether it is expressed in creed or in narrative, in formal statement of belief or in song of praise, God is known and worshiped as Creator and Sustainer of all creation. Here it is important to note that God is Creator in his manifold life as Father, Son, and Holy Spirit.

Although the first chapter of Genesis—as well as other parts of the Bible—emphasizes the creative work of God, this work issues from the trinitarian "community." Thus, in the beginning "the Spirit of God" moves creatively over the waters (Gen. 1:2).[3] And of Christ, the Logos of God, it is said, "All things were made through him, and without him was not anything made that was made. In him was life, and the life was the light of men" (John 1:3, 4). The one God—Father, Son, and Holy Spirit—is the Creator of all of nature; there is no corner of natural reality that is not equally the creative handiwork of the one God who is worshiped as triune being.

The implications of this creedal belief, according to the manifold aspects of biblical revelation, are many. Although most of these elements belong to the remainder of this essay, several things need to be said at the outset of inquiry into a theology of nature:

1. *Created reality has a unity stemming from the unity of God the Creator.*[4] The standpoint of ecological concern is anticipated in this ancient creed that understands the unity of all creation. Naturally, we should not project our own specific ecological understanding onto the author of the original creation narratives, and we ourselves still acknowledge the mystery of creation after careful scriptural and scientific inquiry. But we can see in many ways that the "coinherence" of creation was recognized and celebrated.[5]

2. *All that is is dependent upon God.*[6] Where God "breathes," there is life; where he removes his breath (Spirit), there life ceases (Ps. 104:29). Since all that "is" is dependent upon God, God alone is worthy of worship. It is folly to worship "living things" like trees (Jer. 2:20), just as it is folly to cut down a tree, to carve it, to

---

3. For an exploration of the Spirit in creation, see Hendry, *Theology of Nature*, pp. 140-74.

4. See Walther Eichrodt, *Theology of the Old Testament*, vol. 2, trans. J. A. Baker (Philadelphia: Westminster Press, 1967), pp. 112-13.

5. For a helpful exploration of the useful term "coinherence," see James Houston, *I Believe in the Creator* (Grand Rapids: Eerdmans, 1980), pp. 17-18, passim.

6. Eichrodt, *Theology of the Old Testament*, 2: 97.

decorate it with fine gold, and then to bow down and worship it rather than the one who made the tree and the gold that covers its articulated form (Isa. 44:9-20). One of the insights of more recent analysis of the creation narratives is that they carry on a sharp polemic against the "false gods" worshiped by the pagan neighbors of the Israelites. Biblical writers formulated their narratives in such a way that, again and again, the sun and moon and stars and water and the work of human hands are assigned a secondary place, making them less than God.[7]

3. *God the Creator is understood as a personal, spiritual being whose will not only brings into being all that is, but also sustains it.* God is never an impersonal power whose power is meaninglessly or capriciously dispensed. No, the heavens and the earth are the result of his having exercised his sovereign word—in the same way that he continues to address the human creature through his sovereign words. This encourages the scientist and the theologian who affirm the credo that God is Creator to look for evidences of purpose and intelligibility and meaning in the universe—even as humankind, created in the image of God, so acts, according to constitution and need.[8] The creature who knows the Creator to have and to exercise the attributes of personal will will be sensitive to every evidence of that will, wherever it is manifest. Indeed, we seek (pray for) knowledge of that will and express gratitude (thanksgiving, praise, worship) for the beneficence of the will that sustains our life as well as all of life.

4. *Because God is the Creator of the heavens and the earth and all that is in them, creation is by definition good*—even as God is good (Pss. 25:8; 34:8; 106:1; Mark 10:18). Every reader of the creation narratives will remember the resounding refrain running through the narrative of Genesis 1: "And God saw that it was good" (Gen. 1:12, 18, 21, 25). Indeed, the closing note in the narrative of this chapter reads, "And God saw everything that he had made, and behold, it was very good" (v. 31). This "good, very good"[9] of God has echoed from the lips of humankind down through the centuries. The grandeur of a lofty alpine peak, the

---

7. See Claus Westermann, *Creation*, trans. John J. Scullion, S.J. (Philadelphia: Fortress Press, 1974), pp. 43-45; and Walter Zimmerli, *Old Testament Theology in Outline*, trans. David E. Green (Atlanta: John Knox Press, 1978), pp. 34, 37.

8. For an excellent commentary on purpose, intelligibility, and meaning in creation, see Langdon Gilkey, *Maker of Heaven and Earth* (New York: Doubleday, 1959), pp. 106-77.

9. On this, see Eichrodt, *Theology of the Old Testament*, 2: 108; and Westermann, *Creation*, pp. 60-64.

awesome sweep of the great prairies, the roar of the great waters, the gathering of great flocks of geese, the industry of the ant, the beauty of a rose—all these in their individuality and in their inter-relatedness as minute representatives of the greater creation have been occasions for the divine and human verdict of "good, very good." One wonders how that verdict should be pragmatically applied by humankind to nature. Sadly, we know all too well how often the "very good" has been despoiled of its goodness.

5. *The biblical materials place affirmations of God's (good) creative work alongside recognition of evil in the world.* Not the least of mysteries—perhaps the greatest of mysteries for faith—is the fact of evil in the world. Indeed, so thoroughgoing is the biblical testimony to God's sovereign activity in bringing into being all that is that Karl Barth's description of sin as "the impossible possibility" is particularly apt. Humankind is not only frail, made of dust; it is also sinful. It is not only other than God (and thus dependent upon God); it asserts its otherness in ways that can only be described as rebellion (sin) against God.

No sooner is the work of creation and the ensuing Sabbath rest at an end than the race enters into temptation. The proverb "like father, like son" describes human activity from that point on, manifest in the form of deadly enmity between Cain and Abel. There are at least two messages that reside in this juxtaposition of sovereign creation and sin (against the Creator). First, there will be no facet of creation free from the power of sin. (That power increases if the one bearing the image of God disregards that image.) From the beginning, nature and culture alike have shown the baneful effect of sin upon human life and culture. Second, at the same time, the wise reader of Scripture will remember that the creation narratives and all material attesting that God is Creator belong to the life of a people who have been redeemed by God out of Egypt, who know God as the maker and keeper of a saving, life-giving covenant. In a very real way, the more sin abounds in creation, the more faith knows that God will ultimately triumph over that evil. Our times are in God's hands. Faith is never blind to sin, and never hopeless over against the power of the seemingly overwhelming evil in the world.

The Creation of Nonhuman Life

Although special attention is focused upon the creation of humanity (and its implication for the handling of all creation) in the creation narratives and other aspects of biblical revelation, our interest here also directs our attention to the creation of nonhuman living things—plants, birds, fish, and animals (to follow the order of Genesis 1). All of these are called to bring forth according to their kind (Gen. 1:11-12, 22, 24, 25). Creation is thus presented as a well-ordered whole wherein one can depend upon the continuity of life according to its own bounds and its own kind. As Claus Westermann points out in his book *Creation*, "As long as the earth remains, there can never be a single plant among the hundreds of thousands that exist that does not belong to its own species within this whole. Just because it belongs to its kind, each individual is directed to the ordered whole, God's Creation."[10] Westermann explains that the dependability of kind begetting kind mirrors the dependability of the covenant-making and covenant-keeping Creator of these very things: "Where Yahweh was acknowledged as Creator, it was inconceivable that the creation should be based upon impulsive caprice, or the unpredictable and aimless sport of kindred or hostile or divine powers; the sovereignty of God experienced in the present moment meant that it could only have been transcendent rationality and moral force which determined the character of the created order."[11]

The account of the creation of animals in Genesis 1 differs from that in Genesis 2. In the former chapter, they are generally related to the entire created order; in the latter, they are more particularly related to the creation of humankind. In Genesis 1, animals are differentiated from plants and related to man in that they are *blessed* with the capacity to be fertile and to propagate according to their own kind. Animals also share with humankind and other living beings a common dependence upon the breath of God for life (Gen. 6:17; 7:15, 22; Eccles. 3:19, 21). Moreover, animals are classified along with man as living creatures (Gen. 2:19). But from this point there is a dramatic parting of the ways. It is enough to have observed that the Creator, all of whose work is very good, animates the whole of creation with the very breath of life. Because humankind is similarly (but, in manner, differently) animated, it cannot be indifferent to this fact. We now turn our attention to "the crown of creation."

The Creation of Humankind

A primary concern of theology must be that of determining the proper place of humankind before God, in the context of creation. What is the purpose of God for humankind? What is the relation

---

10. Westermann, *Creation*, pp. 45-46.
11. Eichrodt, *Theology of the Old Testament*, 2: 98.

of humanity to all aspects of creation, animate and inanimate? And what is our required obedience? These questions and others now invite our attention. It is clear that the creation of humankind is a critical concern of the Genesis narrative. It is also clear that the narrative intends first and foremost to praise God as the Creator of all creation and to allow a view of the place of humanity in the glorious sweep of God's creative activity.

More recent scholarship on Genesis has drawn attention to the marvelous way in which the Genesis narrative accents the uniqueness of human creation at the hand of God the Creator. This special privilege and position of humankind is stressed by the following factors (and others) in the narrative:

1. Creation on the sixth day, *after* all other creative work had been accomplished (Gen. 1:31).

2. The unique language with which the divine decision to create is announced. Instead of the impersonal imperative "Let there be," there is a divine statement in the first-person plural: "Let us make man in our image. . ." (Gen. 1:26ff.).

3. The creation of humankind in the image of God (Gen. 1:27).

4. The special emphasis upon human creation as community: "Male and female he created them" (Gen. 1:27).

5. The unique manner in which humans, male and female, are formed—the former from the dust of the ground, with the breath of life breathed directly into his nostrils (Gen. 2:7); the latter with a rib taken from the side of Adam (Gen. 2:21-22).

6. The creation of animate life as a help for Adam (Gen. 2:19); however, these creatures are not seen as the fitting and needed help (Gen. 2:20). One could determine that "good" is not necessarily "good enough" for the crown of creation.

7. The granting to humankind of dominion over all things including all animals, no matter how strong or grand they might be (Gen. 1:28).

8. The formulation of the second creation narrative in such a way that the remainder of animate life is shown to be created for man (Gen. 2:7ff.).

9. Humankind's being granted the responsibility of naming the animals, which are brought before Adam by God himself (Gen. 2:19-20).

10. Above all else, God's direct relationship with and address to humankind as the unique crown of creation (Gen. 1:28ff.; 2:16ff.). That address speaks of fruitfulness, dominion—and the further divine mandate for the way of life in the Garden (Gen. 2:16-17).

More materials and nuancing of the narrative could be noted. This more obvious material is illustration enough of the many ways in which the creation narrative of Genesis underlines the uniqueness of human creation by God. We cannot avoid this fact—but neither may we abuse it. The concern of theological work must be to attend to the ways in which the Lordship of God the Creator is manifest to the human creature, male and female.

One of the most remarkable statements in the Genesis narrative is that the final creative act of God the Creator, who pronounced all the preceding created things "good," was to create humankind in his own image (1:27). It is remarkable that enormous effort has been devoted to interpreting this particular passage and concept, yet there have been such divergent results, most of which miss the obvious. As Westermann has noted in *Creation*, the interpretation of the Genesis narrative and the other related passages has gone astray in the effort to locate the image of God in some quality of humankind rather than in its fundamental constitution. The error has been in failing to pay attention to the image as a holistic reality.[12]

In determining how this larger conceptualization of the image of God illuminates the phrase "image of God," the reader of Genesis must heed the way in which the expression appears in the development of the creation narrative. The dominant impression of the narrative prior to Genesis 1:26 is that God possesses and exercises personal will. The sovereign God determines to create and carries out a series of interrelated creative acts by the power of his will. Because the will of God is perfectly consummated, the continued judgment exercised is "God saw that it was good." Thus, deliberate speaking, observing, judging, and declaring out of the matrix of personal will and power are entirely characteristic of the narrative prior to Genesis 1:26.

The flow of the narrative prior to this point virtually forces the conclusion that humankind *in the image of God* in 1:26 will be a personal being other than and less than God, invested with the attributes of speaking (and hearing), observing (knowing, understanding), judging, and pronouncing. This is in fact the case in the ensuing narrative. The one created in the image of God hears God and speaks to God, observes the creation of God within the context of the Garden, makes judgments about that creation (naming animals; judging that it is not true that death will follow disobedience to the voice of God), and declares the names of animals that God passes in review. The point is that humankind is differentiated from all other entities God has created in that the very prerogatives of God are, in some measure, mediated to this

---

12. Westermann, *Creation*, pp. 55-60.

crowning work of creation. The miracle of creation is that God places his imprint upon the dust of the earth, thus filling human life with the vitality of divine breath and promise. The divine gift is simultaneously awesome benefaction and challenge. The human creature, created in the image of God, then receives multiple privileges and mandates:

"Be fruitful and multiply, and fill the earth" (1:28).

"Subdue it . . . and have dominion" (1:28).

"The Lord God took the man and put him in the garden of Eden to till it and keep it" (2:15).

"You may freely eat of every tree of the garden" (2:16).

"But of the tree of the knowledge of good and evil you shall not eat" (2:17).

"I will make him a helper fit for him" (2:18).

"The Lord God formed every beast of the field and every bird of the air, and brought them to the man to see what he would call them; and whatever the man called every living creature, that was its name" (2:19).

Humans are like God in that the created order is uniquely for them, meant to provide them with something to use and enjoy, something over which to exercise dominion. Likewise, it is the privilege of humankind to be in relationship to God and co-humanity and to animate life. Also, the spoken word of humankind, like that of God, has a unique power—albeit one granted by God.

When humankind sins, it is not so much "the image of God"—some inner "attribute"—that is lost, but humanity itself that is lost. The Fall is best understood as the loss of that full relationship to (fellowship with) God correspondent to the divine purpose, as well as the loss of vitality given (and taken) in "the breath of God." (Ultimately, death follows disobedience.) Finally, the earth and its creatures come to stand in an ambiguous relationship to humanity, being sustained by God, independent of human effort (indeed, human effort is sustained by creation), but nonetheless suffering as a result of human disobedience to the Creator.

In *Creation* Westermann underlines the fact that the first three chapters of Genesis reveal only part of the author's intention; the full account of human origins has not been heard until Genesis 1-11 has been heard in its entirety.[13] Like his analysis of

---

13. Westermann, *Creation*, pp. 21-31.

the meaning of creation in the image of God, his contribution here has the strength of inviting readers of Genesis to see the obvious—which is typically missed in the interpretation of Genesis 1-11. Although Genesis 1-3 is an object of frequent attention in Christian reference to the Old Testament, it is a fact that Genesis 4-11 is too little read and very little understood.

Among other things, Westermann shows how the Flood narrative is to be related to the creation narratives. Basically, the fact of God's creative work means that he also has in his hand the power to destroy. The promise of God "never again to destroy the life which he had created 'as long as the earth remains'" means that the creature receives from the Creator the promise of preservation—that is, the promise of providential care.[14] But there is a warning over all this: "Man, just because he has been created, carries within him limitation by death as an essential element of the human state. . . . The Flood narrative also indicates quite clearly that the history of mankind will have an end. The catastrophe at the beginning points to the catastrophe at the end. The interlude is the time of preservation. . . . We see here the correspondence between primeval time and end time."[15]

Westermann also points out a number of significant aspects of the narrative structure of Genesis 1-11. There are several structural features that are especially noteworthy. In the first place, there is a remarkable correspondence between the promise of blessing and the genealogies: the genealogy of chapter 5 corresponds to the blessing of 1:28, and the genealogy of chapter 10 to the blessing of 9:1. In the former pair, blessing works itself out in chronological succession; in the latter it is effective in territorial expansion. There is yet another "fulfillment" of blessing (we have noted the commissions to "fill the earth and subdue it" [1:28] and "to till and keep" the Garden [2:15]):

> The dynamism of the blessing which is man's because he is a creature of God is realized in work. It is not something fixed and rigid; rather, there belongs to its very nature a process of growth which expresses itself in the diversity of kinds of work and in the progress and accomplishments of civilization. . . . The commission to work leads to the division into the two basic ways of life, the agricultural-sedentary and the nomadic, and as a result comes the building of cities, art (musical art first), and technology. Attention is then drawn to the possibility that, because of the increase in the

---

14. Westermann, *Creation*, p. 22.
15. Westermann, *Creation*, p. 22.

achievements of civilization and progress in technology, a sense of power is attained that can lead to overstepping the limits and to mistakes.[16]

The ways in which these limits are overstepped follow in rapid succession in Genesis 1-11. They include the disobedience of Adam and Eve in the garden (3:1ff.), the murder of Abel by Cain in anger (4:8ff.), the arrogance of Lamech (4:23-24), the consorting of the sons of God and the daughters of men (6:1-14), the continually evil thoughts of humankind (6:5), the general corruption and violence of humankind (6:11-12), the sin against the nakedness of Noah by his son Ham (9:20ff.), and the arrogance of humankind in building a tower "with its top in the heavens" (11:1ff.). Again and again humankind ungratefully abuses and violates the original gifts and privileges it was granted. Dominion is forced upon humankind as well as animals. Knowledge is shamefully misdirected; life is destroyed; humankind is full of evil rather than goodness. Rather than being subject to God, humankind usurps the prerogatives of God. By the end of chapter 11, the reader knows that humankind, though called to be earthkeeper in the fullest meaning of this word, earth being the creation of God, is prone to violate that trust. Nonetheless, God has entrusted the earth to no one else. But there is another One, the Image of God, who comes to redeem humankind, and to point to and enable "a better way."

Jesus Christ, the Image of God

One of the points consistently made by recent statements on the meaning of creation in the Bible is that creation provides the context for (biblical) history. Thus creation and redemption, or creation and covenant, are always interrelated in biblical perspective. Although the connected themes are not extensively displayed in the New Testament, the nexus of redemption history and creation is powerfully stated when it does appear. The supreme instance of that interrelationship is located in the Incarnation. For Jesus Christ is seen as the uniting agent, the Redeemer-Creator entering into creation. The Gospel of John and the Epistle to the Colossians provide striking statements of this connection:

> In the beginning was the Word, and the Word was with God, and the Word was God. He was in the beginning with God; all things

---

16. Westermann, *Creation*, pp. 25-26.

were made through him, and without him was not anything made that was made. In him was life, and the life was the light of men. The light shines in the darkness, and the darkness has not overcome it.

(JOHN 1:1-5)

He is the image of the invisible God, the first-born of all creation; for in him all things were created, in heaven and on earth, visible and invisible, whether thrones or dominions or principalities or authorities—all things were created through him and for him. He is before all things, and in him all things hold together.

(COL. 1:15-17)

Line after line of these two passages calls the hearer back to the creation narratives of Genesis. Whatever other explicatory reference is to be seen, the reference to Genesis remains certain.

These passages raise a question (which cannot be answered here in any detail): How does the image of God in Christ relate to the image of God in humankind referred to in Genesis? An excerpt from the article on creation in the *Interpreter's Dictionary of the Bible* offers this explanation:

> In Jesus Christ, God has restored the human pattern intended at the original creation. . . . He is the new humanity into which man may be born, not through biological parentage, but by his decision in response to divine grace. Thus the Christian community, from the standpoint of faith given by God's revelation in Christ, looks backward and forward. It traces God's purpose to the first creation, saying: "In Christ all things were created"; and it lives toward the future, saying: "God will sum up all things in Christ."[17]

Our review of the image of God in Genesis reminded us of the importance of seeing the image as a whole. The truth and the meaningfulness of that image come to rest in Christ, although with the difference that he is the full and perfect expression of God, truly *"the* image of the invisible God"—not simply *in* the image of God.

We now turn our attention to the value of this truth in the Incarnate Christ. If Christ is "the image of God" in the fullest sense of the term, what does the incarnate ministry teach us with respect to our posture in and toward creation, with special reference to creation/nature? Once again we are forced to reduce a

---

17. Bernard W. Anderson, "Creation," *Interpreter's Dictionary of the Bible*, 4 vols., ed. George Buttrick (Nashville: Abingdon, 1962), 1: 732.

large subject to a brief sketch, albeit a critical sketch for Christian belief with respect to creation and nature. Following is a list of some of the more prominent features of the Gospel narratives, a list limited to the Synoptic Gospels because of the repeated, parallel witness to Jesus' work and words therein. The Gospels (among others) ground these perspectives in Jesus, and in his mission and message:

1. God is the Creator of this world and all that is. Indeed, in Jesus the whole of creation is transparent to God.

2. The providential care of God is everywhere evident in the world; God keeps his creation covenant with the very birds of the air (Matt. 6:26).

3. The dependability of God is written into nature (see the structure/assumptions of the parables).

4. God's creation is a good and beautiful creation (Matt. 6:28-29), and therefore an occasion for enjoying the goodness of God's provision for us (Mark 2:18–3:6).

5. Despite the fact that nature gives evidence of the handiwork of God, evil power has intruded into the world of nature (see the miracles that, on behalf of humankind, reverse evil in nature).

6. Despite the goodness of what is, it is not to be assigned a place of dominion in human life (Luke 12:32-34; see also Jesus' own denial of self/things, as in the Temptation).

7. Nature's divinely grounded "goodness" allows its fruit to be a sacrament of the kingdom and presence of God (Mark 14:22-25).

There is much more that could be said. However, suffice it to say that Jesus is always paradoxically at home in this world but not possessed by it. He who is the very image of God lived comfortably in the world but as though its form were passing away (see 1 Cor. 7:31). What matters is that we reflect on the creation of human life in the image of God with the true image of God before us.

HUMANKIND AS EARTHKEEPER OF CREATION

We are now in a position to describe the meaning of a biblical theology of nature/creation for a Christian theology of nature with special reference to current ecological concerns. In doing so, we reject the position that the biblical injunctions in the creation narratives of Genesis have been *the* cause of a wrongheaded view and use of nature.

The biblical revelation offers no basis for a course of human action that leads to ecological disaster. Indeed, as will be seen, the whole of biblical revelation points in the opposite direction. The problem with our human approach to nature is kindred to the problem that Albert Schweitzer once observed regarding critical perspectives on the historical Jesus: Everyone tends to interpret Jesus according to the bent of his or her own philosophy or religion. This often happens, the more so the closer something lies to one's heart. Since nature's "goods" are often all too close to our hearts, it is easy for us to hear the biblical revelation as we will, and not as the Spirit wills. We may respond with an individual act or a corporate act.

There are basically two ways of getting at the matter of humankind as earthkeeper of creation. One is to make a theoretical beginning, going back to "the beginning." The other is to begin where we are in the history of the world, with many human resources already badly threatened, and with countless species of animals, birds, reptiles, fish, insects, and all manner of plant life already vanished. The first perspective is entirely theoretical, and we cannot return to it now except in a piecemeal fashion at certain points on the globe. The second perspective seems to offer no way to gain an upper hand, given the enormous population of the world coupled with the enormous and growing consumption of the world's goods. Nonetheless, the human creature lives in creation and is subject to the Creator who formed it in the beginning and who sustains it. This is an inescapable privilege and responsibility, and there we must begin. In any effort we make to deal with nature today, it is important that we—who are both threatening it and sometimes threatened by it—be guided by a number of understandings:

1. *God is the sovereign Creator and Sustainer of the universe.* Because God remains sovereign, because his personal will is at work in the creation, we will not make the mistake of believing that we can do the work of God, whether in a positive or a negative sense. Humankind does not in itself have the resources or the power to recreate the good earth—nor the power to destroy the earth. Both these powers belong to God. Earthkeepers will always be sensitive to the will of the Creator God who gives and who takes away, but who has sustained the earth according to his covenant from the beginning. Whatever the human powers of destruction may be in a theoretical sense, humankind, created in the image of God, is called upon to emulate in real actions the sustaining will of God with respect to the "good" creation.

2. *Humankind is called to be fruitful, but also to be responsible.* When fruitfulness in terms of population increase endangers the

existence of our neighbor, near or far, now or in the future, we are called to rethink our ideas regarding procreation. The celibate life of Jesus shows us that procreation is not determinative for humanity. The fact is, however, that a large percentage of the Christian population has not believed this in the past and does not believe it now. Since increase in one's own life now means the death of one's brother in the future, we are not far removed from Genesis 4 and the story of Cain and Abel. Or do our "neighbors" belong to our present generation alone?

3. *Humankind is called to responsible dominion over all creatures of the earth, creatures that are a part of God's good creation.* How can we deny what has been a fact for virtually the whole of recorded history: that humankind has increasingly exercised dominion over creatures (now, for all practical purposes, over all creatures)? Dominion, however, does not mean mistreating single exemplars or destroying a whole species. There is not the slightest allowance for such a tendency in the biblical narratives. In their distinctiveness, all created entities are a cause for wonder. In their unity, they are a part of the unity of creation, a unity that is a given, a unity whose destruction leads to the ecological disasters that are increasingly evident in many quarters of the globe. Dominion means "responsibility for" before God, not "irresponsibility toward" before God. Dominion in the image of God is the exercise of servanthood to the Ruler of all nature.

4. *"The fruit of the earth" is given to humankind for nourishment and strength.* Here again, we cannot deny what has been a fact for the whole of human existence. We are somehow especially dependent upon the fruit of the vine and the field. Perhaps we need to explore that "original word" today. Although Israel was not averse to enjoying meat, it is a fact that the creation narrative points to a vegetarian diet as the principal mode of human sustenance. Today we are disturbed by the large amounts of vegetarian foodstuffs fed to animals raised for meat while many fellow humans go hungry, and thus we may be inclined to force the text in Genesis to advocate vegetarianism. But to do so would suppress the other line of biblical teaching, which surely sanctions the eating of meat—indeed, the meat offered in connection with slain sacrifices to God. Genesis 1:29, however, may be allowed to point us to the better way in this time of global hunger. The call to denial of self needs to inform all aspects of existence—including our diet. Such denial may increasingly be the needed "good news" for starving humanity and also for the assaulted earth.

5. *Human work and efforts toward civilization are a part of the*

realization of full humanity and should not be automatically counted as an assault against nature. The biblical teaching concerning humankind and nature is not simply an invitation for the race to return to the wilderness—if this were possible. Indeed, at this juncture of civilization, given the bad manners of "civilized" people, most of humanity will need to learn much about the care of the earth in order to live with nature, whether in its "pure" form (wilderness) or otherwise. It is important to accept this outfitting for culture, but we must also recognize that this embrace of our full humanity raises problems for maintaining the unity, balance, goodness, and beauty of nature. Life is always lived out in this tension— fruitful tension, it is hoped—between the enjoyment of wonder and the enjoyment of "the good things of the earth" conveyed to us through human effort.

6. *There is no reason to suppose that sin, which lurks always at the door of human existence, will ever be absent from human concourse with nature.* Although, strictly speaking, one would not speak about sins against nature, without question human sin repeatedly has an impact upon nature, whether direct or indirect. Greedy exploitation can unwisely denude whole regions of trees, with the result that other vegetation, creaturely life, and the earth itself suffer. The widespread desire to sport certain animal furs in public places—although there are more comfortable and economical ways to keep oneself warm and protected—has led to the virtual extermination of many species of animals. Is there any way in which humanity can justify such actions? Can anyone believe that the good creation of God was intended for such usage? Unfortunately, these are modest offenses when compared with certain global practices that often amount to a wholesale rape of nature and natural resources of all kinds. The violation of the limits established for human existence leads to the diminution of the very world in which human life is sustained.

7. *Such is the result of the divine constitution of the earth that humankind needs nature more than nature needs humankind.* The Creator has put the earth at the disposal of humankind, not the reverse. The result, however, is that every diminution of nature's capacity to serve its intended purpose is ultimately a threat to humankind. To presume upon nature is finally to presume upon God, who gives us nature as an envelope for life as well as a place that provides sustenance and meets all kinds of human needs. Ultimately, the earth provides the context for human history; without the earth, there is no history. On a diminished earth, history itself is altered. And this alteration is an alteration of

humanity at the individual, the corporate, and the universal levels.

8. *The pattern of Genesis, mirrored elsewhere in the Bible, still offers the penultimate and positive pattern of human regard for nature.* We are called to understand (and name) the animals, and to till and keep the earth. We are called to be fruitful—but also to realize that the Creator has ordained that *all* living things should be fruitful. This means that humanity must coexist with nature in a symbiotic relationship of mutual fruitfulness. We are called to recognize with God that every created thing is, in its own way, good and beautiful. This leads us away from willful disregard and destruction (but does not call us to foolish toleration of that which is destructive to the human race). This will even lead to efforts to sustain parts of the creation in its original form, to pass it on to the next generation as the same gift from God received from the past. Wilderness is a great gift; it is unthinkable that humankind should not protect this exemplar, nature's original, as a gift from God that has been and should remain a part of human history.

9. *The creation is an invitation to wonder and the praise of God.* Throughout the Psalms (though not only there), the praise of God for his goodness, might, and wisdom is manifest as the appropriate human response to God's creative activity, experienced especially as the world of nature around us. There are some things that humankind cannot change—but the perspective and the experience of them can be so altered as to diminish the awe that they elicit. When mountains are barely visible through a dense pall of smog over the valleys below, they surely elicit less wonder than they do on a clear day, the kind of day antedating recent efforts toward "civilization." It is passing strange that whereas civilization has caused humanity to bring out the inner music, visions, and stories of the race, it has not caused us to similarly prize and nurture the wonders of creation that are perennially evident, even though natural "wonders" are more universally regarded as objects of "wonder" than the products of human hand and mind. The work of theology has come full circle when we experience deeply the invitation to wonder, and understand more deeply exactly why this should be so.

A PRAYER FOR CREATION

We have been taught to pray for all manner of things. (For all that, an overwhelming portion of our prayers is too often limited to more "personal" concerns.) The creation narratives and our passing reflection on them suggest the need to pray for creation. This may seem odd; how many prayers have you heard for creation other than such limited ones as those asking God to keep it from raining, or making some other whimsical request?

Why should we pray for creation? Will not God take care of creation? The question, on reflection, proves to be foolish. For God takes care of his people, but those people are also to be objects of our prayerful concern. God will bring in his kingdom, but we are still invited—by the Lord—to pray for the coming of this kingdom. Indeed, we are called to make "common cause" with God in prayer for all things God is doing. It is the desire of our heavenly Father that we should join our spirits with his Spirit in prayerful response to all that he is doing and will do.

God is at work—still—in creation. It is right and good that we should make the entire created order—humankind being simply a "peak" manifestation of the created order—a constant object of prayer.[18]

We need especially to entreat God's forgiveness for raping creation. Indeed, we need to pray for strength to resist participation in the communal rape of nature that is going on all about us. Too often we are partners in this evil, whether consciously or unconsciously. Our prayer should arise from a life attuned to the call of Jesus Christ, the image of God, who discerned the hand of God in nature always, and took no more of nature's bounty than was needful for daily life. This One teaches us to pray today, "Thy will be done, *on earth* as it is in heaven."

---

18. For an injunction to pray for creation and its creatures, great and small, see Agnes Sanford, *Creation Waits* (Plainfield, N.J.: Logos International, 1977).

Stewardship of the Earth in the Old Testament

WILLIAM DYRNESS

I

In the West there has been a tendency to begin discussions of human responsibility toward the earth with statements of the centrality of the person. The earth is made for man and woman, we are told, and only when these do their part can the earth properly praise God. Teilhard de Chardin is perhaps the most important thinker to argue along these lines. "With hominisation, in spite of the insignificance of the anatomical leap, we have the beginning of a new age," he says. "The earth 'gets a new skin.' Better still, it finds its soul."[1]

This idea of humanity as the convergence of all the processes of creation has been more recently argued by T. F. Torrance. He insists that there is a profound harmony between the rationality of the universe and that of human understanding.

WILLIAM DYRNESS (D.Th., University of Strasbourg) is President of New College, Berkeley, a Christian graduate school of integrative studies for the laity. Previously he taught for eight years in the Philippines. He has written on various issues of theology and culture. His latest book, Let the Earth Rejoice: A Biblical Theology of Holistic Mission *(Crossway Books, 1983), provides a biblical framework for thinking about ecology.*

---

1. Teilhard de Chardin, *The Phenomenon of Man* (New York: Harper's, 1959), pp. 182-83.

Humanity "is given a special place within the creation with a ruling and a priestly function to perform toward the rest of created reality. All lines of rationality and order of purpose of fulfillment . . . [which] converge on him as man of God and man of science depend on his destiny."[2] Not surprisingly, when these thinkers discuss responsibility toward the earth, they relate it primarily to a development of the human project, which is God's highest end of creation. They believe, furthermore, that the development of modern science follows as a natural consequence of this Christian and biblical view of things.

When science and technology proved hazardous to our environment, there were those quick to point to this line of thinking as a cause for much of the difficulty we had gotten ourselves into. The criticism of Lynn White, Jr., is the most famous of a number of attempts to blame this Christian view of creation and human domination—"the Christian axiom that nature has no reason for existence save to serve man"—for the growing ecological crisis.[3] He was simply taking seriously Christian thinkers who had long argued that it was the Old Testament and the Christian view of creation that gave birth to modern science.[4] But while he may well have followed other Christian thinkers in this assessment, there are those who feel that he did not take the Old Testament data with sufficient seriousness. Dick Wright, a biologist, has argued that White's whole attack is a misreading of the Old Testament accounts.[5] James Barr, an Old Testament scholar, has gone even further, claiming that the whole supposed connection between science and the Old Testament is faulty and needs to be rethought. If Hebrew culture contained the germ of modern science, he points out, one would have expected some minimal distinctiveness in science and technology to have characterized the material life of ancient Israel. But this is exactly what one does

---

2. Torrance, *Divine and Contingent Order* (New York: Oxford University Press, 1981), p. 129. See also Torrance, *The Ground and Grammar of Theology* (Belfast: Christian Journals Ltd., 1980), chap. 1: "Man, the Priest of Creation."

3. White, "The Historical Roots of Our Ecological Crisis," *Science*, 10 March 1967, pp. 1203-7. See also Ian McHarg, *Design with Nature* (Garden City, N.Y.: Natural History Press, 1969).

4. See as representative R. Hooykaas, *Religion and the Rise of Modern Science* (Grand Rapids: Eerdmans, 1972); and Alfred North Whitehead, *Science and the Modern World* (New York: Macmillan, 1925), p. 19.

5. Wright, "Responsibility for the Ecological Crisis," *Bioscience*, 1 August 1970, pp. 851-53.

not find. What is there seems simply continuous with the understandings of Israel's neighbors.[6]

In his inaugural address at Oxford, John MacQuarrie pointed out the complexity of Hebrew thinking about the world. While there is in the Old Testament a monarchical view of human relationship to the earth, there is also a more organic view in which God and the world are not strictly separated. This view was similar to that which developed in Greek philosophy and which, by giving a higher place to nature, was able to enlarge our knowledge of mathematics. This organic view, MacQuarrie believed, was completely displaced by the monarchical model and the nominalism of the Middle Ages, which may well have given rise to the exploitative attitude toward the earth.[7]

The following examination of the teaching of the Old Testament will show that the generally asymmetrical view of the relation of humanity to the earth is quite properly being questioned, and that a more organic relationship may be more appropriate. In fact, in the Old Testament view, both creation and humanity must be understood as created by God to be testimonies to his goodness in their interaction. That is, the earth was created so that something may happen between God and his creation, something that is called the covenant in the Old Testament and that comes to full expression in the Incarnation of Christ. Man and woman—in their creation and their mandate to have dominion over the earth—are obviously central to the creation, but this is rigorously qualified by their covenant responsibilities. Far from demeaning the natural order or human responsibility toward creation, this view puts these things in their proper perspective and gives them their full value.

II

Human responsibility toward the earth must begin with the recognition that God, not human effort, gives fertility to the earth. Already in Genesis 1, before the creation of man and woman, God instructs the waters and the earth to produce living creatures, and all of them to "be fruitful and multiply" (vv. 20, 22, 24). All the way through Genesis (and the Old Testament), this theme is

---

6. James Barr, "Man and Nature—The Ecological Controversy and the Old Testament," *Bulletin of the John Rylands Library* 55 (1972-73): 9-32.

7. MacQuarrie, "Creation and Environment," *Expository Times* 83 (1971-72): 4-9.

sounded like a refrain: the blessing of God issues in the fertility of land, livestock, and people.

> The Lord has blessed my master abundantly. . . . He has given him sheep and cattle, silver and gold (Gen. 24:35).

> Isaac planted crops in that land and the same year reaped a hundredfold, because the Lord blessed him (Gen. 26:12).

> The blessing of the Lord was on everything Potiphar had, both in the house and in the field (Gen. 39:5b).

> [God] makes grass grow for the cattle, and plants for man to cultivate—bringing forth food from the earth (Ps. 104:14).

Fertility and offspring are gifts of the earth that represent the blessing of God. There is every encouragement to enjoy this goodness; there is no indication that it can be earned. The commission of the man and the woman to have dominion must be understood in this context. The blessing of the earth is nowhere premised on the proper exercise of that dominion; in fact, God must bless the human creation just as he has blessed the rest of creation (see Gen. 1:28). It is God who makes them fruitful, just as he has made all creation fruitful before them.

When God commands the man and the woman to "rule" or have dominion, it is in the context of this God-ordained order and productivity. The earth is not waiting for them to bear its fruit, though it is waiting for them to lead creation to its higher ends. But what then is the nature of this "rule" over creation? Since the word is that generally used of the rule of a king, I believe the key is to be found in the unique conception of "rule" that is developed in the Old Testament and that is specifically applied to Israel's kings. Deuteronomy 17:14-20 points out that Israel's king is to rule as a brother over brothers and sisters, is not to accumulate large amounts of gold, and is to read and meditate on God's word "so that he may learn to revere the Lord his God and follow carefully all the words of this law" (v. 19). These injunctions are in complete contrast to the concepts of the ancient Near East. Here is an organic rather than a strictly monarchical view of kingship and ruling, one that is further illumined in the life and ministry of Christ, who came not to be served but to serve (Mark 10:45). The rule that men and women are to exercise over creation, then, is one of servanthood, as a brother or sister "rules" over others in the family.

This conception is further explained in the second (and probably earlier) account of creation in Genesis 2:4ff. Here the Garden is already planted and growing when the man is placed in it "to work it and take care of it" (v. 15). The Hebrew words used here are most interesting. The first *(abad)* means to work in the sense of serving. The noun derivative, in fact, means "slave" or "servant." The second *(shamar)* implies a watchful care and preserving of the earth. The responsibility of the man, it seems, is to serve and watch over the earth to preserve—rather than to produce—its goodness. The other specific activity Adam is given corroborates this sense of rule: God brings him the animals and birds to see what he will name them. In doing this the man is to order them and confirm their meaning, just as God has ordered and named the day and the night in Genesis 1:5.

If my thesis—that human dominion is best seen in the ideal rule of Israel's king—is valid, then we should expect that the righteous rule of the king would issue in a productive and fruitful environment, both human and nonhuman. And in Psalm 72, the great hymn of praise for the righteous king, this is precisely what we find:

> Endow the king with your justice, O God,
>> the royal son with your righteousness.
> He will judge your people in righteousness,
>> your afflicted ones with justice.
> The mountains will bring prosperity to the people,
>> the hills the fruit of righteousness. . . .
> Let grain abound throughout the land;
>> on the tops of the hills may it sway.
> Let its fruit flourish like Lebanon;
>> let it thrive like the grass of the field.

> *(Vv. 1-3, 16)*

This rule is both a reflection of God's own righteous rule and an expression of God's purposes for all who bear his image and exercise his dominion. It is precisely this rule and this image that is embodied in Christ, who showed his concern for the poor, multiplied the loaves and fishes, and calmed the sea. Moreover, according to the New Testament view, this image can now be shared by all God's people as the Spirit is poured out on all, from "the least to the greatest" (Acts 2:17 and 18, where Peter is quoting Joel 2:28-29).

Clearly, goodness and fertility are assumed to be natural characteristics of the earth, and the man and the woman are merely to facilitate and enjoy this bounty. Furthermore, God doesn't give any clear guidelines as to how this is to be done. In fact, when the man is placed in the Garden (Gen. 2:15) and told to care for the earth, the only instruction that he receives is that though he may enjoy any tree he likes, he must not eat from the tree in the center, or he will surely die. Here the guidance is religious and not secular. In secular matters he is on his own, enjoying the freedom of the children of God to play and work according to their gifts—to observe and discover the order God has created. We will want to return to this point later.

III

The close interrelation between humanity and the natural order is underlined in the Fall, described in Genesis 3. Rebellion against God disrupts relationships among people and between people and the land. When the man and the woman fall into sin, the earth is cursed because of them, or for their sakes (v. 17). Now it must be tilled and harvested through painful toil, and, God says, "it will provide thorns and thistles for you" (v. 18). This could mean that the man and the woman would do something wrong, or exercise their dominion in such a way that the earth would bear thistles, but we are not told that this is so. Rather, the implication is simply that there is now something wrong with the order of things that will show itself in ecological misfortunes. And this state is directly related to God's own interest in creation and the human response to him and his instructions. In some way man and woman have become enemies of the creation (Gen. 9:2).[8] Israel was solemnly warned later when she entered the land: "Even the land was defiled; so I punished it for its sin, and the land vomited out its inhabitants. . . . And if you defile the land, it will vomit you out as it vomited out the nations that were before you" (Lev. 18:25, 28).

But even now that the land begins to share the distortion that human sin introduced, there is no special interest taken in methods or procedures for caring for the land. As James Barr notes, in Genesis "there is little interest in the development of tools and weapons."[9] This is not to say the earth plays no part in

---

8. In *A Worldly Spirituality: The Call to Take Care of the Earth,* Wes Granberg-Michaelson argues that the Flood changed the relationship between people and animals: animals became fearful of the now-predatory men and women. He points out, too, that the covenant God now makes includes a promise to preserve the earth—once again, God's work rather than a human burden (San Francisco: Harper & Row, 1984), pp. 78-79.

9. Barr, "Man and Nature," p. 25.

the early program of God: the earth is cursed by a flood because of human sin (Gen. 7-9), and it is central to covenantal promises made to Abraham (12:1 and 17:8). But few guidelines for its care are given.

Like creation, the land of Canaan is blessed—flowing with milk and honey—before the entrance of God's people. When the Israelites come into the land, however, no special emphasis is placed on how they are to care for the earth. Clearly the assumption is that they will practice good stewardship. Their responsibility for their inheritance is inviolable. The response of Naboth to King Ahaz is indicative of this sense of solidarity: "The Lord forbid that I should give you the inheritance of my fathers" (1 Kings 21:3). When they plant any fruit tree, they must leave it alone for four years, "but in the fifth year you may eat its fruit. In this way your harvest will be increased. I am the Lord you God" (Lev. 19:25). When they lay siege to a city, they are not to destroy the trees "because you can eat their fruit" (Deut. 20:19).[10] Land is to be left fallow every seventh year because "the land is to have a year of rest" (Lev. 25:4, 5). And "when you reap the harvest of your land, do not reap to the very edges of your field or gather the gleanings of your harvest. Leave them for the poor and the alien. I am the Lord your God" (Lev. 23:22).

This last reference points up the difficulty of separating instructions about care for the land from those concerning care for people (or animals!). But this is to be expected if all alike reflect God's single blessing, a state that is identified with *shalom* (peace) in the Old Testament (cf. Isa. 55:12; Mal. 2:5). Overall, the instructions belong to the general body of wisdom of the ancient Near East, and seem to be no special possession of Israel. What is special about these instructions is that they are tied to the unique position that Israel holds and are punctuated with the reminder "I am the Lord." The Israelites' stewardship is to reflect the fact that the land belongs to God and that they are only caretakers of it (Lev. 25:23). God assures them that if they will hear his voice and serve him with all their heart, "then I will send rain on your land in its season, both autumn and spring rains, so that you may gather in your grain, new wine and oil. I will provide grass in the fields for your cattle, and you will eat and be satisfied" (Deut.

---

10. This admonition "not to destroy" became central to Jewish commentaries that outline environmental regulations. Granberg-Michaelson discusses these in *A Worldly Spirituality*, pp. 83-84.

11:14, 15). True, they are to be wise in their stewardship, to tend the earth and make it bear fruit. This common wisdom is a gift of God. But even in this they are to "remember the Lord your God, for it is he who gives you the ability to produce wealth, and so confirms his covenant" (Deut. 8:18).

When a farmer plows for planting, does he plow continually?
Does he keep on breaking up and harrowing the soil?
When he has leveled the surface, does he not sow caraway
    and scatter cummin?
Does he not plant wheat in its place, barley in its plot, and
    spelt in its field?
His God instructs him and teaches him the right way.

(ISA. 28:24-26)

IV

We have already observed how difficult it is to make methods of care for the earth an object of independent research in the Old Testament. One is continually brought up against the fact that morality, response to God, and fertility of the earth are interrelated. We noted above that when Adam is placed in the Garden, a point at which one might have expected God to give a little advice about care for the property, God gives instruction that reflects his own Lordship and the necessity of Adam's response to that. Here is the central drama of creation, in which the earth is fully involved. One almost has the impression that if this order is respected, the fruitfulness of the earth will be more or less a natural consequence. The implication is that the created order has more than a natural function; it also has an expressive or symbolic purpose that relates it to the purposes of God. Indeed, H. Wheeler Robinson points out that the Hebrew had no way of rendering nature, the "creative and regulative physical power," other than by using the word "God."[11] Methods and procedures cannot be made an object of independent (would we say objective?) research simply because these things are always expressive of God's purposes. "Did not Israel," Gerhard von Rad asks, "in all her attempts to perceive the course of human experience, always come back to God who comprehended all things in his power?

---

11. Robinson, *Inspiration and Revelation in the Old Testament* (New York: Oxford University Press, 1946), p. 1.

There was never a special domain in which she was alone with her understanding and the objects of her knowledge."[12]

The fact that the elements and processes of nature are taken up into the larger purposes of God is illustrated by the complex and apparently irrational dietary and defilement laws of Leviticus. Of the numerous attempts to interpret these instructions, two seem to predominate: the one attempts to make them medicinal in nature; the other sees them as merely arbitrary. While the former is neither a consistent nor comprehensive interpretive program, the latter abrogates interpretation altogether. Besides, as Mary Douglas points out, Leviticus is certainly an unexpected place to find arbitrariness, since the paramount concern of the priestly writer is order. There must be some way to understand these instructions in relation to the overall order of creation, which we are to reflect in the whole of our lives.

Douglas has explained this in her book *Purity and Danger: An Analysis of Concepts of Pollution and Taboo*. "In the Old Testament we find blessing as the source of all good things," she points out, "and the withdrawal of blessing as the source of all dangers. The blessing of God makes the land possible for men to live in." In creation God has created an order in which men and women (and the entire natural order) may prosper. This blessing is preserved as men and women keep covenant with God and follow the order he has specified. Thus these instructions are "efficacious and not merely expressive." The precepts are all focused on the idea of holiness and wholeness that people are to reflect (and create) in their lives. "Livestock, like the inhabited land, received the blessing of God. Both land and livestock were fertile by the blessing, both were drawn into the divine order. The farmer's duty was to preserve the blessing." Holiness, then, is given physical expression in various laws. The injunction to maintain bodily purity and wholeness, the forbidding of hybrids (i.e., confusion of the order), the identification of certain animals as unclean because they deviated from the "pure types" of the three animal spheres—these functioned "like signs which at every turn inspired meditation on the oneness, purity and completeness of God . . . and would thus have been a meaningful part of the great

---

12. Von Rad, *Wisdom in Israel* (Nashville: Abingdon Press, 1972), p. 72. Compare this with A. R. Peacock's statement: "The world of matter in its relation to God, has both the symbolic function of expressing his mind and the instrumental function of being the means by which whereby he effects his purpose" (in *Man and Nature*, ed. H. Montefiore [London: Collins, 1975]).

liturgical act of recognition and worship which culminated in the sacrifice in the Temple."[13]

All of this becomes clearer when seen in the light of the creative purposes of God in the Old Testament. All of God's work involves the earth, humankind, and divine purposes in intimate interrelationship. All involve creating order in place of chaos. Creation is pictured, especially in the images of Psalm 89, as wresting meaning out of disorder. In the Exodus God moves his people from slavery, through wilderness, into the order of productivity of Canaan.[14] Even in the Exile God offers hope of a future exodus in which the desert will bloom again. In their obedience God's people are to reflect this divine ordering in their human way.

This last period of Old Testament history is so important that it bears closer examination. We have seen that the rebellion of God's people consistently resulted in barrenness, beginning in the Garden of Eden and continuing right up to the settlement. Part of the explanation for the ban on the Canaanite cities, and the ecological disaster that brought about, was their wickedness (see Gen. 15:16; Lev. 18:25). So when the land again becomes barren and the people are sent away into exile, there can be only one fundamental explanation for it: "Your children who follow you in later generations and foreigners who come from distant lands will see the calamities that have fallen on the land and the diseases with which the Lord has afflicted it. . . . All the nations will ask: 'Why has the Lord done this to the land?'. . . And the answer will be: 'It is because this people abandoned the covenant of the Lord. . .'" (Deut. 29:22, 24, 25).

But the judgment that God brings upon the land is not an arbitrary curse. It is exactly the reverse of what he had intended for his people. Since he is the righteous Creator God, the real fertility God (see Hos. 2), his people who reflect his image are to reflect his creativity and his care in their lives and communities. As Moses promises in Deuteronomy 28, "If you fully obey the Lord your God and carefully follow all his commands I give you today, the Lord your God will set you high above all the nations

---

13. Douglas, *Purity and Danger* (New York: Praeger, 1966), pp. 45-46, 50, 54, 57.

14. See the excellent study of Walter Brueggemann, *The Land* (Philadelphia: Fortress Press, 1977). I have integrated this into a theology of mission in *Let the Earth Rejoice: A Biblical Theology of Holistic Mission* (Westchester, Ill.: Crossway Books, 1983).

on earth. . . . You will be blessed in the city and blessed in the country. The fruit of your womb will be blessed, and the crops of your land and the young of your livestock—the calves of your herds and the lambs of your flocks" (vv. 1, 3, 4).

None of this would happen as a matter of course. The Israelites had to carefully observe God's instructions, which included (as we have seen) general principles of moderation and wisdom. These common-sense rules and instructions should not be underestimated; their elaboration and development is fully laid out in the wisdom literature of the Old Testament (and the comparative literature of the ancient Near East). But all of this belonged to the natural wisdom with which people were created. It was expressive of the rule they were designed to enjoy in the created order, a rule that was to have great consequence for the natural environment, and that was to be pictured above all in the rule of Israel's king.

However, hope for this kind of rule in the Old Testament grows progressively dim. And the resulting unfaithfulness is inevitably accompanied by the ruin of the earth and its resources. Clearly, just as wisdom and careful stewardship are the natural counterparts of righteousness and obedience to God's order, so foolishness and waste become characteristic of a disobedient people:

They trample on the heads of the poor as upon the dust of
    the ground
        and deny justice to the oppressed. . . .
I will tear down the winter house along with the summer
    house;
        the houses adorned with ivory will be destroyed. . . .
I also withheld rain from you. . . .
Many times I struck your gardens and vineyards,
        I struck them with blight and mildew. . . .
I sent plagues among you.

(Amos 2:7; 3:15; 4:7, 9, 10)

Again we observe the complex of disobedience to God, oppression of the poor, and ecological disaster. The one cannot be separated from the other in the Old Testament. One cannot selfishly pursue physical prosperity (Amos writes during the second golden age of Israel under the rule of Jeroboam II) without courting long-term disaster for the people and the land.

God promises these curses as a clear response to unfaithfulness, both religious and ecological. But the terms in which they are portrayed are most interesting. As Michael Deroche points out, these judgments are pictured as an exact reversal of God's creative acts.[15] As God has populated the earth, so he will de-populate it:

"I will sweep away everything from the face of the earth,"
    declares the Lord.
"I will sweep away both men and animals;
    I will sweep away the birds of the air
    and the fish of the sea."

(ZEPH. 1:2, 3)

Notice that animals, birds, and fish are swept away in exactly the opposite order in which they are listed in Genesis 1:28. Human rule has been perverted because of unfaithfulness, and thus creation has been unmade. Since God had made a covenant that includes the whole earth in its purview, Israel's unfaithfulness will have world-embracing consequences. In Hosea the "case" that God makes against this people specifies that they no longer show faithfulness, love, and the knowledge of God—all covenant stipulations.[16] And as God has gathered his people, so he will scatter them. And the earth will be barren.

If there is any doubt about human responsibility for the earth and its preservation, these prophetic books should remove it. God is saying through these prophets that the very stability of the created order is dependent upon Israel's faithfulness to the covenant. As Deroche puts it, "If Israel breaks the covenant by following the idolatrous practice of the nations, God's creation will be uncreated."[17]

Not that the prophets eliminate all hope for the earth. Quite the contrary. Just when things seem the bleakest, when all seems lost, specific promises for the land shine the brightest. But note that God must intervene and perform still another act of creation, or bring about another exodus. In fact, as J. A. Baker notes, "As hopes pinned on human rulers are falsified, the vision of a world of abundance and peace becomes a part of a hope set on God alone."[18] As God at the first had to make the earth fruitful, so he

---

15. See Deroche, "The Reversal of Creation in Hosea," *Vetus Testamentum* 31 (1981): 400-409.

16. Deroche, "The Reversal of Creation in Hosea," pp. 400-409.

17. Deroche, "The Reversal of Creation in Hosea," p. 407.

18. Baker, "Biblical Attitudes to Nature," in *Man and Nature*, ed. H. Montefiore (London: Collins, 1975), p. 93.

will again work and bring about a situation in which abundance will be possible:

> On the day I cleanse you from all your sins, I will resettle your towns, and the ruins will be rebuilt. The desolate land will be cultivated instead of lying desolate in the sight of all who pass through it. They will say, "This land that was laid waste has become like the garden of Eden."
>
> *(Ezek. 36:33-35)*

> The desert and the parched land will be glad;
> the wilderness will rejoice and blossom.
> Like the crocus, it will burst into bloom;
> it will rejoice greatly and shout for joy.
> The glory of Lebanon will be given to it,
> the splendor of Carmel and Sharon;
> they will see the glory of the Lord,
> the splendor of our God.
>
> *(Isa. 35:1, 2)*

Though hope comes to rest in God alone, his people are fully involved in the realization of these purposes. Of the images that point to this fact, I mention two.

First, in Jeremiah 29:5-7, Jeremiah gives some very interesting instructions to the people living in exile in Babylon: "Build houses and settle down; plant gardens and eat what they produce. Marry and have sons and daughters; find wives for your sons and give your daughters in marriage. . . . Increase in number there; do not decrease. Also, seek the peace and prosperity of the city to which I have carried you into exile. Pray to the Lord for it, because if it prospers, you too will prosper." Though God has judged them, and as a consequence their land is barren and they are childless, they are to begin again to exercise the rule that God originally gave them in Genesis 1:28. In this way they can recreate the earth and spread the knowledge of the Lord, and so enjoy the blessings of the earth.

The second image is the promise (or instruction) that in that day they will beat their swords into plowshares. The importance of this expression is underlined by the fact that the combination is quoted three times in the prophets. In Isaiah 2:4 it is associated with the invitation of the last days to come up to the mountain of the Lord to walk in his ways. In Joel 3:10 the reverse command is contained in a proclamation to the nations that stands as a judgment of them. As a part of the final battle with the forces of evil, the nations are called on to beat their plowshares into swords.

Micah seems to be quoting the Isaiah passage in a similar context (4:3). The phrase is obviously meant to display an antithetic parallelism. Plowshares clearly stand for the facilitating rule that people are called upon to exercise as God's image bearers. The obverse of this is symbolized by the sword, wherein the disorder and destruction introduced by human unfaithfulness have taken control. Joel 3 implies that God will judge this unfaithfulness by employing this very disorder, but meanwhile he calls his people to reflect his own righteous rule in their lives and communities.

V

Before we draw these observations together, there is another aspect of creation that must be examined. If we are right in seeing God's purposes as central to the created order and as our calling to reflect the order of these purposes in our lives, we are also relieved of the pressure to make creation at every point useful for human society. One of the ironies evident in the Book of Job is that these "philosophers" feel called upon to explain all that is happening to Job in a very modern way. But in chapters 38-40 God makes it clear that there is much that cannot be comprehended in their explanations. In this large-minded picture of creation, the great fish sports in the ocean and the animals play: "Who has a claim against me that I must pay? / Everything under heaven belongs to me" (41:11).

All that God has made exists for his own purposes, which often transcend our human point of view. Here lies a great justification for the preservation of wilderness areas that exist for no other purpose than to exhibit the greatness of God by preserving his creative work. This is also the explanation for the sense of exaltation that so many people feel when they share in this untouched beauty. The universal reaction to such pristine beauty is that one feels close to God, or whatever universal power one believes in. Here more than any other place we are sharing in God's own delight in his handiwork, the delight that moved him to say in the beginning, "It is very good."[19]

VI

We have found that we cannot abstract principles of ecology and stewardship from the theological complex in which they are

---

19. I owe this observation to my brother, Dr. C. T. Dyrness, Director of the Institute of Northern Forestry in Fairbanks, Alaska.

found. God has created the world as a place where righteousness and beauty will be established. But this involves a system of relationships—among God, his people, and the land—which are all included in the covenant God has established with the earth. There is every encouragement to use wise methods of stewardship, though this is more often assumed than debated. But these are a part of a larger response to God's covenanting love. When we respond in obedience, we will enjoy the fruit of the earth, and the poor will be cared for. When we turn from God, we can expect ecological disaster and social oppression. And this is precisely what history and our own experience attest.

Though we learn great respect for the earth from the Old Testament, in the end Lynn White, Jr., and the Sierra Club will not be happy with what we find there. We find serious environmental problems addressed—wells are filled in, groves of trees are cut down. But these are discussed as part of a larger problem that involves the purposes of God and human rebellion against these purposes. Moreover, there is no indication that our environmental problems can be addressed apart from this larger problem. If any blame is to be laid for the present challenges, we must place it here. Biologist Dick Wright puts it this way: "There is no need to search the past to find the basis . . . for [human] exploitation and misuse of nature. The explanation reveals itself every day, if we care to look for it, because it is present in each of us—human greed, carelessness, and ignorance."[20] This is especially true if we see these characteristics institutionalized in the habits and structures that make society what it is.

Proper stewardship of the earth, then, is a matter of recovering the creative rule that God intended people to exercise toward the natural order. This is a rule that involves a proper husbanding of resources so that they will produce enough to care for the needs of all, and a respect for the order as accomplishing purposes that transcend even our understanding. Fertility has something to do with care of the poor; both have to do with God's loving purposes for the earth. Our calling is to reproduce in our human way these purposes.

A central Jewish understanding of epistemology is that all intellectual activity is a dialogue with God at Sinai, an "attempt to discern more clearly how to respond to His command."[21] If this is

---

20. Wright, "Responsibility for the Ecological Crisis," p. 852.
21. Myron B. Bloy, Jr., *Religion in Intellectual Life*, Fall 1983, p. 5.

so, all human thinking has ecological implications. For it is surely a passionate exercise that includes all the responses to God's commands here discussed in an effort to make this world—especially its physical environment—a concrete image of the world to come.

Wisdom Literature and Its Contribution to a Biblical Environmental Ethic

ROBERT K. JOHNSTON

Then God said, "Let us make man in our image, after our likeness; and let them have dominion over the fish of the sea, and over the birds of the air, and over the cattle, and over all the earth, and over every creeping thing that creeps upon the earth." So God created man in his own image, in the image of God he created him; male and female he created them. And God blessed them, and God said to them, "Be fruitful and multiply, and fill the earth and subdue it; and have dominion over the fish of the sea and over the birds of the air and over every living thing that moves upon the earth."

GENESIS 1:26-28

The starting point for a biblical environmental ethic is the cultural mandate, humanity's God-given dominion over the wider creation. Yet such a starting point has caused as much confusion as help, as much grief as joy. According to Wes Granberg-Michaelson, Genesis 1:28 has become the proof text of the

ROBERT K. JOHNSTON *is Dean and Associate Professor of Theology and Culture at North Park Theological Seminary in Chicago. A graduate of Stanford University, Fuller Theological Seminary, and Duke University, he taught at Western Kentucky University and New College, Berkeley, before assuming his present position. Johnston is the author of* Evangelicals at an Impasse: Biblical Authority in Practice *(John Knox Press, 1979),* Psalms for God's People *(Regal, 1982), and* The Christian at Play *(Eerdmans, 1983). He has also published articles and reviews in the* Reformed Journal, Catholic Biblical Quarterly, Christian Century, Christianity Today, *and* Theology Today, *among others.*

"industrial age's attitude toward the resources of creation. Adam Smith and Karl Marx alike have regarded nature as nothing more than the warehouse supplying the raw materials for the transformation of society and history."[1]

With Granberg-Michaelson, most of us realize that the abuse of our natural resources is not justified by the creation texts. What is not clear, however, is what exactly is encouraged. Only men and animals are mentioned in regard to humankind's dominion. What of vegetation? geology? the oceans? the wider universe? How are we to interact with the environment in which God has placed us?

If we would understand the full intention of the creation text that speaks of humankind's dominion over the animal kingdom, if we would find a responsible biblical perspective toward the whole of nature, then we must look beyond the creation texts themselves to their biblical commentary: the writings of Old Testament wisdom literature. For as Walther Zimmerli has convincingly argued, "Wisdom thinks resolutely within the framework of a theology of creation."[2] Or, as David Hubbard puts it, "Theologically wisdom has as one of its functions an explication of Genesis 1-2. It is part of the out-working of the God-given commands to subdue the earth and name the animals. Understanding the creation is not merely a means of success for man, it is a divinely designed way of blessing. By acquiring and applying wisdom, man fulfills one of the purposes for which he was created."[3]

Yet even here we must be cautious. Questions abound even while we broaden our inquiry concerning a biblical environmental ethic. By using the term "wisdom literature," are we forcing otherwise disparate materials into a common mold and thus skewing the interpretation? Some question whether there was a distinct wisdom movement in Israel, although texts like Jeremiah 18:18 lend support to its reality. ("Then they said, 'Come, let us make plots against Jeremiah, for the law shall not perish from the priest, nor counsel from the wise, nor the word from the prophet.'") Also, what is the extent of Old Testament wisdom literature? Three books (Proverbs, Job, Ecclesiastes)? Five (the

---

1. Granberg-Michaelson, "At the Dawn of the New Creation," *Sojourners*, Nov. 1981, p. 15.

2. Zimmerli, "The Place and Limit of the Wisdom in the Framework of the Old Testament Theology," *Scottish Journal of Theology* 17 (1964): 148.

3. Hubbard, "The Wisdom Movement and Israel's Covenant Faith," *Tyndale Bulletin* 17 (1966): 22.

previous three plus the Song of Songs and selected Psalms)? Or seven (the previous five plus Ecclesiasticus and the Wisdom of Solomon)? Are the forms and substance of wisdom thought to be found in other parts of the Old Testament, too (the Joseph narrative, Isaiah, additional Psalms, and so on)? That is, is wisdom to be found in the law, the prophets, and the larger writings as well? The concept of wisdom literature is inescapably vague.

Even more difficult to delimit is the term "wisdom" itself. In one of his last major contributions, *Wisdom in Israel*, Gerhard von Rad recognized that "the concept 'wisdom' has become increasingly unclear."[4] It does not help that the ancient Hebrew and the modern English definitions are various and often quite distinct. As I have noted elsewhere, "for both the ancient Hebrew and the modern English-speaking individual, 'wisdom's' range of overlapping and at times contradictory meanings extends from craftiness to sagacity, from erudition to common sense."[5] Thus we cannot simply transfer our ways of thinking about wisdom to the biblical text. Nor can we look at any single text in isolation from the larger biblical witness.

Despite such cautions, however, an analysis of Old Testament wisdom literature can be a fruitful enterprise for the person interested in ecology. For, as Zimmerli points out, wisdom is *"per definitionem taḥbūlôth,* 'the art of steering,' knowledge of how to do in life, and thus it has a fundamental alignment to man and his preparing to master human life."[6] First, wisdom literature is instructive in its focus upon creation, both in its nature wisdom and in that wisdom which is humanly oriented. Second, rooted in experience, wisdom literature models both a particularity and an openness. Third, seeking to order life, it avoids concepts of reason that stress power and the ability to control, basing its knowledge instead on mutuality and trust. In each of these regards, it is important to stress at the outset that wisdom literature is never merely secular. Wholly involved in the world and responsible for his/her destiny, the wise person knows of no reality outside of the nurturing control of Yahweh.

---

4. Von Rad, *Wisdom in Israel*, trans. James D. Martin (Nashville: Abingdon Press, 1972), p. 7.

5. Johnston, "Redefining 'Wisdom,'" *Journal of the American Scientific Affiliation* 34 (1982): 44.

6. Zimmerli, "The Place and Limit," p. 149; cf. Gerhard von Rad, *Old Testament Theology*, vol. 1, trans. D. M. G. Stalker (New York: Harper & Row, 1962), p. 421.

FOCUSED UPON CREATION

The fourth chapter of 1 Kings describes Solomon's wisdom in these words:

> And God gave Solomon wisdom and understanding beyond mea-
> sure, and largeness of mind like the sand on the seashore, so that
> Solomon's wisdom surpassed the wisdom of all the people of the
> east, and all the wisdom of Egypt. For he was wiser than all other
> men . . . and his fame was in all the nations round about. He also
> uttered three thousand proverbs; and his songs were a thousand
> and five. He spoke of trees, from the cedar that is in Lebanon to the
> hyssop that grows out of the wall; he spoke also of beasts, and of
> birds, and of reptiles, and of fish.
>
> *(Vv. 29-33)*

It is not Solomon's ability to render justice—not even his ability to rule effectively—that is highlighted in this summary text concerning his wisdom. Rather, it is his encyclopedic knowledge of his environment. This is all the more striking when one turns by way of contrast to the Book of Proverbs. There the focus is on human life and experience. Although Israel is said to have culti-vated a nature wisdom in Solomon's day, in the canonized tradi-tion (the Old Testament Scriptures) this material has been almost totally suppressed.

The Old Testament does, however, retain a few examples of nature poems, which in the diversity of their content and form suggest a once-vibrant wisdom tradition. The speeches of God in the Book of Job (chapters 38-41) concerning the snow and the rain, Pleiades and Orion, the ostrich and the horse, the hippopotamus (Behemoth) and the crocodile (Leviathan) are one such example. So too are Psalm 104 and the numerical sayings in Proverbs 30:18-19, 24-31 (cf. as well the series of natural phenomena men-tioned in Sirach 43:1-25). These texts are similar to wisdom writ-ings that could be found in both Egypt and Mesopotamia. According to Albrecht Alt, "Toward the end of the second millen-nium B.C. this *Gattung* of wisdom [nature wisdom] was definitely alive in quite similar form in both Babylonia and Egypt, can-onized in the former while still productive in the latter."[7]

---

7. Alt, "Solomonic Wisdom," trans. Douglas Knight, in *Studies in Ancient Israelite Wisdom*, ed. James L. Crenshaw (New York: KTAV Publishing House, 1976), p. 108.

Von Rad has observed as well the similarities between the passage in Job 38-41 and the learned patterns evidenced in the Egyptian *Onomasticon of Amenemope* (approximately 1100 B.C.).[8] There is no direct borrowing asserted, but rather a free poetic adaptation of this encyclopedic work.

Solomon's wisdom—that which was said to surpass the wisdom of both Egypt and Mesopotamia—was evidenced in his ability to adapt a pregiven tradition of "enumerative science" to a radically altered poetic form that allowed these materials to express even the worship of Yahweh. By expanding the bare enumerations of the nature lists (a protodictionary) into a whole series of proverbs and songs (possibly as many as 3,000 proverbs and 1,005 songs), Solomon was able to present relationships in the natural world that could not be expressed by means of the traditional listings. In particular, as von Rad has argued, Israel was able to adapt this "somewhat arid scientific material to the purposes of the worship of Yahweh."[9] In both form and content, then, Solomon's treatment of the world about him surpassed the wisdom of his day. This is what attracted the Queen of Sheba (1 Kings 10).[10]

A particularly striking example of Israel's adaptive use of nature wisdom is the hymnic praise of Psalm 104. Although not a wisdom piece per se, it has its source in the wisdom materials of its day. In his article entitled "Observations on the Creation Theology in Wisdom," Hans-Jürgen Hermisson points out that just as Solomon made proverbs "from the cedar that is in Lebanon to the hyssop that grows out of the wall" (1 Kings 4:33), so one may find in Psalm 104 "the same assignment of beings to their local and temporary realms: the badger to the rocks, the stork to the cedar trees, the lion to the night, and man and his work to the day." Hermisson continues: "Naturally, then, there is more here than the mere compilation of creatures and environments. The meaningfulness of such coordination becomes evident, too: in this world and its manifold spaces everything is well arranged ecologically."[11] As the writer of Proverbs 16:4 (Solomon?) suggests, "The Lord has made everything for its purpose."

---

8. Von Rad, "Job XXXVIII and Ancient Egyptian Wisdom," in *The Problem of the Hexateuch and Other Essays* (London: Oliver & Boyd, 1965), p. 287.

9. Von Rad, "Job XXXVIII and Ancient Egyptian Wisdom," p. 287.

10. R. B. Y. Scott, "Solomon and the Beginnings of Wisdom in Israel," *Vetus Testamentum Supplement* 3 (1955): 267.

11. Hermisson, "Observations on the Creation Theology in Wisdom," in *Israelite Wisdom: Theological and Literary Essays in Honor of Samuel Terrien*, ed. John

Psalm 104 begins by describing the heavenly activities of the Creator (vv. 1-4), how he made the earth (vv. 5-9) and continues to irrigate and tend it (vv. 10-13). God is said to provide more than just what is needed. Wine gladdens the heart, and oil makes the face shine (vv. 14-16). God appoints how and where all creatures are to live—in the air (v. 17), on land (vv. 18-23), and in the sea (vv. 24-26). All living beings are totally dependent upon him (vv. 27-30). Surely the Lord's name is to be praised (vv. 31-35).

Several observations can be made concerning this hymn. First, it portrays the world in such a way that there is a meaningful order for all time and space, creatures and things. There is an overarching harmony within all creation. This ordered world is not autonomous, however. It exists solely because of the continuous care of its Creator and Sustainer. Here is a picture of creation that extends the Genesis accounts. It presents God planting the cedars, watering them, and populating them with birds. As Hermisson notes, "Passages like the ones we find in this Psalm do not merely encourage recognition that man must care for the earth; they underscore the fact that *God* cares for *His* earth."[12] Encyclopedic lists could not portray the grandeur of this ordering of all creation and of its Orderer. Indeed, only this hymnic form of presentation could open the reader to a proper devotion, a rejoicing in the Lord who showers his continuing devotion on his creation.

Second, Psalm 104 provides commentary on the creation accounts by portraying the importance of rocks and trees, birds and animals for their own sake. Creation does not exist only for the sake of "man." According to Hermisson, "Everything has a meaning—even such a bizarre creature as Leviathan out there in the distant ocean whom God created as his toy."[13] And Walter Harrelson observes, "The creative and powerful anthropocentrism of biblical religion is here beautifully qualified: God has interest in badgers and wild goats and storks for their own sakes. He has interest in trees and mountains and rock-cairns that simply serve non-human purposes."[14] Some animals live without reference to us. Others interact with humankind, but still have

---

Gammie, Walter Brueggemann, W. Lee Humphreys, and James Ward (Missoula, Mont.: Scholars Press, 1978), p. 48.

12. Harrelson, "On God's Care for the Earth: Psalm 104," *Currents in Theology and Mission*, Feb. 1975, p. 20.

13. Hermisson, "Creation Theology in Wisdom," p. 48.

14. Harrelson, "On God's Care for the Earth," p. 20.

their distinct spheres of life. Our work is significant, but so too is the lions', "seeking their food from God" (v. 21). Humankind's dominion over the earth is never to be at the expense of God's ongoing creation. We need both ships plying their trade *and* Leviathans playing and cavorting in the sea (v. 26).

Third, this hymnic commentary on creation is not naively out of touch with reality. It is never hopelessly idealistic, even while praising God's overarching design. For the Psalmist is aware of the limits of his (and our!) knowledge and activity. He calls us to enjoy the beauty of creation with its symmetry and interlocking unity. Yet he recognizes the enigmas that remain, both in nature and within humankind. The Lord rejoices in his work, but he also causes the earth to tremble and the mountains to smoke (v. 32). Moreover, there remains the disturbing presence of the wicked, the sinner (v. 35). The Psalmist knows of misery, injustice, and pollution. The world is not what it should be. He pleads with God for "the wicked [to] be no more" (v. 35). Yet his thoughts are dominated not by what is, but by what was and what is to be. The intention of creation is his focus, as Harrelson points out: "The poet has portrayed the world as God made it to be, and he calls upon his hearers to recognize that if such a life is to be theirs, they had better sing and pray, had better recognize that this is how God will have the world be."[15]

* * *

The previous discussion notwithstanding, it would be a mistake to limit our discussion of wisdom literature's focus on creation to the "nature" texts.[16] For even when the emphasis is directed more specifically toward "man," Zimmerli is correct in positing for it "the framework of a theology of creation." In his seminal article "The Kerygma of the Book of Proverbs," Roland

---

15. Harrelson, "On God's Care for the Earth," p. 22.

16. In *Wisdom in Israel*, von Rad is correct to caution against the use of terms like "nature wisdom." Israel did not think in abstractions, whether "nature," the "world," or "life." Von Rad writes, "Israel was not aware of this or that entity which we almost automatically take as objects of our search for knowledge. . . . She did not differentiate between a 'life wisdom' that pertained to the social orders and a 'nature wisdom,' because she was unable to objectify these spheres in the form of such abstractions" (p. 71). There is an immediacy and a concreteness that informs the entire wisdom movement. Nevertheless, just as scholars recognize two forms of wisdom literature, proverbial (Proverbs) and contemplative (Job), so too we can speak of two subject matters, nature and humankind.

Murphy argues that "the kergyma" is life itself.[17] The instructions of the book are meant to offer impetus and direction concerning the shape and maintenance of life as it was intended by God. As Dame Wisdom exhorts,

> And now, my sons, listen to me:
>> happy are those who keep my ways.
> Hear instruction and be wise,
>> and do not neglect it.
> Happy is the man who listens to me,
>> watching daily at my gates,
>> waiting beside my doors.
> For he who finds me finds life
>> and obtains favor from the Lord;
> but he who misses me injures himself;
>> all who hate me love death.
>
> *(PROV. 8:32-36)*

In the Book of Proverbs, wisdom offers her invitation repeatedly. Standing in the streets at the city gates where all will pass by, she makes her appeal (8:2-3). Hers is a "path of life" (2:19; 5:6; 10:17); her teaching, a "fountain of life" (13:14; 16:22). There is a strong value judgment expressed by the term "life."[18] Length of days (3:16), a good name (10:7), riches and honor (22:4), God's presence (21:30)—all are part of life's definition. "The wage of the righteous leads to life, the gain of the wicked to sin" (10:16; cf. 11:19; 12:21).

The value of life as created by God is again evident in the Book of Ecclesiastes. Providing further commentary on the Genesis creation accounts, the writer picks up such creation motifs as human nature returning to dust (12:7; cf. Gen. 2:7), man inclined to sin (7:20; cf. Gen. 3), woman as companion (9:9; cf. Gen. 1:27), knowledge as limited (8:7, cf. Gen. 2:17), life as "good" (2:24; cf. Gen. 1), and toil as tiring (1:3; cf. Gen. 3:14-19). Although the book centers on our inability to discover the secret of life's meaning, it also admonishes its readers to enjoy life as a gift from God, the Creator: "Go, eat your bread with enjoyment, and drink your

---

17. Murphy, "The Kerygma of the Book of Proverbs," *Interpretation* 20 (1966): 9.

18. Murphy, "The Kerygma of the Book of Proverbs," p. 10. Cf. Gerhard von Rad, "Zaō," in *Theological Dictionary of the New Testament*, vol. 2, ed. Gerhard Kittel, trans. G. W. Bromiley (Grand Rapids: Eerdmans, 1964), p. 843.

wine with a merry heart; for God has already approved what you do" (9:7; cf. Gen. 1:31, where God declares everything he has made to be "very good"). With Robert Gordis, I would understand the "basic theme of the book" to be "*simḥah*, the enjoyment of life."[19] Although we cannot master life, given the limits imposed on human experience, "the preacher" would nevertheless argue for our active participation and engagement in the world. As Walter Brueggemann points out, "Life has been called good (Gen. 1:31). . . . It is for our enjoyment, celebration, application."[20]

ROOTED IN EXPERIENCE

Axiomatic is wisdom literature's orientation within the framework of a theology of creation. Several corollaries follow from this, the chief of which is wisdom literature's rootage in experience. This experiential focus is not to be interpreted as "secular" or "profane" in contrast to the "sacred" orientation of the law and the prophets. All of life was understood as stemming from God. The wise men would not have conceived of the possibility of any reality not controlled by God. Thus victory comes not simply because of an "abundance of counselors" (Prov. 24:6) but because it "belongs to the Lord" (Prov. 21:31). It is not only "the teaching of the wise [which] is a fountain of life" (Prov. 13:14). It is not only "he who is steadfast in righteousness [who] will live" (Prov. 11:19). It is also "the fear of the Lord [which] prolongs life" (Prov. 10:27). To the Israelite, "wisdom," "steadfastness in righteousness," and "fear of the Lord" were interchangeable, though not synonymous, concepts. It is perhaps this fact that allowed wisdom and law to eventually be identified as one in Sirach 24. Surely this fact lies behind the oft-repeated proverb "The fear of the Lord is the beginning of wisdom" (Prov. 9:10; cf. Prov. 1:7; 15:33; Ps. 111:10; Job 28:28).

Yet, although none of the wisdom materials is lacking at least a wider Yahwistic context (given, if no other indication, their canonical location), von Rad is right in suggesting that "according to the convictions of the wise men, Yahweh obviously dele-

---

19. Gordis, *Koheleth—The Man and His World*, 3rd ed. (New York: Schocken Books, 1968), p. 131. Cf. Johnston, "'Confessions of a Workaholic': A Reappraisal of Qoheleth," *Catholic Biblical Quarterly* 38 (1976): 16-17.

20. Brueggemann, "Scripture and an Ecumenical Life-style," *Interpretation* 24 (1970): 14.

gated to creation so much truth, indeed he was present in it in such a way that man reaches ethical *terra firma* when he learns to read these orders and adjusts his behaviour to the experiences gained."[21] That is, the argument of wisdom literature is from human experience. Here is the basic source of its authority. We are still dealing with God's revelation to his people, but now there is no claim of an oracle or vision, as with the prophets. Rather, revelation comes from seeing how life works. As David Hubbard states, "Wisdom literature takes human experience and distills it."[22] There is in wisdom the full confidence that creation will reveal its truth to those who open themselves receptively to it, for that is what it has repeatedly done.

Wisdom's experiential focus has several specific consequences relevant to an environmental ethic. First, it precludes dogmatism. Wisdom's horizontal conception of revelation encourages continued observation and reflection. "There is no *office* which gives sanctions to these teachings," writes Brueggemann. "There is only the authenticity of the statement itself, only an invitation, only a 'try it and see.' The validity of the teaching rests upon the fact that life really happens that way. There is no other court of appeal. The teachings simply assert that life is like that! Authority is based only on seeing it as it is."[23]

This lack of dogmatism is apparent in certain proverbs that describe life "as it is" without sanctioning the perspective (e.g., Prov. 17:8: "A bribe is like a magic stone in the eyes of him who gives it; wherever he turns he prospers"). It is also evident in the repeated juxtaposition of different and conflicting teachings, each valid in its particular way. The consecutive proverbs on silence illustrate this:

He who restrains his words has knowledge,
    and he who has a cool spirit is a man of understanding.
Even a fool who keeps silent is considered wise;
    when he closes his lips, he is deemed intelligent.

(Prov. 17:27-28)

So too these observations on speaking to a fool:

---

21. Von Rad, *Wisdom in Israel*, p. 92.
22. Hubbard, lecture delivered at Fuller Theological Seminary, Pasadena, Calif., 2 Jan. 1980.
23. Brueggemann, *In Man We Trust: The Neglected Side of Biblical Faith* (Atlanta: John Knox Press, 1972), p. 18.

> Answer not a fool according to his folly,
>> lest you be like him yourself.
> Answer a fool according to his folly,
>> lest he be wise in his own eyes.
>
> *(Prov. 26:4-5)*

Each proverb is based on careful observation, but together they suggest a fundamental ambivalence toward the events of life. As von Rad points out, "Israel, with great openness, gave precedence to the contingent event over the *logos* achieved by means of abstract calculation. . . . Every sentence was, in principle, open to any possible amplification."[24]

An interesting extension of this nondogmatic orientation is the frequency of an experiential base for the motives given to the exhortations. There is rarely anything axiomatic about them. The motivations seem to be included for practical reasons and lack the weight usually attached to general ethical norms. Proverbs 23:20-21 provides an example:

> Be not among winebibbers,
>> or among gluttonous eaters of meat;
> for the drunkard and the glutton will come to poverty,
>> and drowsiness will clothe a man with rags.

Proverbs 22:9 provides another:

> He who has a bountiful eye will be blessed,
>> for he shares his bread with the poor.

Here we encounter pedagogy grounded in common experience and particular perspective. There is no interest in "theoretical knowledge"; rather, Israel's wisdom literature seeks to provide a specific, pragmatic orientation. This is a second consequence of wisdom's experiential reference.

This eschewal of the theoretical may be illustrated by the notion of "the good" that pervades Proverbs. The good is not abstract but active. The good has a constructive function; it is life-enhancing, as Proverbs 3:27 shows:

> Do not withhold good from those to whom it is due,
>> when it is in your power to do it.

A third consequence of wisdom's rootage in experience is an openness, a certain liberality in viewpoint. There is in all of

---

24. Von Rad, *Wisdom in Israel*, p. 311.

wisdom's admonitions an element of dialectic. Because the teaching of wisdom is not authoritative command but advice, it is discussable. The reader must be free to decide whether the instruction has validity. As von Rad explains, "The man who listens, who reflects and who then entrusts himself to his perceptions; that is the highest form of human existence in the eyes of the wise men."[25] For this reason, perhaps, most of the wisdom sayings take the more neutral form of a statement and not an admonition.[26]

The Books of both Job and Ecclesiastes evidence this fundamental openness within the wisdom movement. Whereas the writer of Proverbs has a certain confidence that the good will be rewarded and the evil punished, Job questions this belief, striking a blow for divine mystery and sovereignty. The Book of Job can be understood as an effort to call the wisdom movement to judgment in order to purify it. The dealings of God with man had become too easily categorized in traditional sayings. Divine liberty was at stake, for many believed God *must* reward the good. Theology was threatened by the profit motive. Theodicy became a challenge to divine sovereignty. In this situation, where God is judged according to our own standards rather than vice versa, the Book of Job asserts divine independence and freedom. We cannot portray God in terms of an ideology of ethical righteousness. We cannot risk boxing him into a particular theory of justice. He is free to act as he will.

The writer of Ecclesiastes similarly questions those who would close in wisdom's observations, turning them into indubitable laws. Written late in Israel's history, Ecclesiastes wages a frontal assault on all misguided attempts to master life by pointing out life's limits and mysteries. If the "art of steering" through life (Prov. 1:5) was permitted to degenerate into cold calculation and toil, then life's depth and grace would be robbed of its charm. Thus the writer of Ecclesiastes challenges those who believe that life opens up before us like a problem to be solved. It cannot be dissected and analyzed, only looked at appreciatively and enjoyed gratefully. Given that death is our common lot (6:6), that

---

25. Von Rad, *Wisdom in Israel*, p. 310.

26. Berend Gemser, "The Spiritual Structure of Biblical Aphoristic Wisdom," *Homiletica en Biblica* 21 (1962): 3. Cf. Roland Murphy, "The Interpretation of Old Testament Wisdom Literature," *Interpretation* 23 (1969): 293: "The appeal is ultimately to the reality which confronts the individual person. Hence they are *ēsāh* (advice), not *dābār* (word)."

God's mysterious plan is inscrutable (3:1-14), and that life is amoral (4:1-2), all "toil" at controlling life is vain. We cannot reduce life's richness to a series of prescriptions. We must instead enjoy our portion as a gift from God (2:24-26; 3:12-13, 22; 9:7-10). He is free to respond as he chooses.

Nondogmatic, concrete, and open to revision and elaboration, Israel's experiential wisdom encouraged a basic humility. Perceptions were never built into a comprehensive system. Phenomena were never objectified but were viewed concretely and particularly. Some questions were never answered except by encounter with the Answerer (cf. Job 38-42; Ps. 73). The contingent was viewed as more fundamental than the abstract. There was a recognition that human insight was in constant need of reworking and reapplication.

> Do you see a man who is wise in his own eyes?
> There is more hope for a fool than for him.

This saying—Proverbs 26:12—is but one of several that suggest that the biblical wise men understood their own limitations well. Proverbs 21:30 is another:

> No wisdom, no understanding, no counsel,
> can avail against the Lord.

As Murphy points out, "This caution is in accordance with the nature of a saying which frames only a limited aspect of reality. The way was never really secure: 'sometimes a way seems right to a man, but the end of it leads to death!' (Prov. 16:25)."[27]

SEEKING TO "ORDER" LIFE

"Biblical wisdom issues from the effort to discover order in human life," writes Roland Murphy. "This thesis is held by so many scholars that it seems to be one of the 'assured results.' "[28] Yet Murphy seeks rightly to qualify such a formulation. Was there really such a philosophical stance or presupposition among the ancient wise men of Israel? Was there an attempt at mastery over

---

27. Murphy, "Wisdom—Theses and Hypotheses," in *Israelite Wisdom: Theological and Literary Essays in Honor of Samuel Terrien*, p. 35. Cf. James L. Crenshaw, "Wisdom in the Old Testament," in *The Interpreter's Dictionary of the Bible, Supplementary Volume*, ed. Keith R. Crim (Nashville: Abingdon Press, 1976), p. 954: "The Fundamental Promise of Wisdom Is Belief in Order."

28. Murphy, "Wisdom—Theses and Hypotheses," p. 35.

life? Did humans seek those hidden orders within the confusion of life's experiences that would make living easier as well as profitable?

In an earlier article on Ecclesiastes, I pointed out the "subtle but profound difference in viewing wisdom as the *'art of steering'* as opposed to 'the *task* of mastering life.' "[29] One is an aesthetic phenomenon; the other, an ethical one. One observes orderliness; the other seeks to impose order. Yet this distinction is too often overlooked. Thus, on the one hand, von Rad argues that "the teachers here are working out only one perception with great keenness: constitutive for man's humanity is the faculty of hearing. If he is not constantly listening to the order established by God, then he is lost."[30] On the other hand, von Rad summarizes wisdom's intention by saying, "There was surely one goal, to wrest from the chaos of events some kind of order in which man was not continually at the mercy of the incalculable."[31] This kind of inconsistency in perspective produces a certain ambiguity in the analysis of many commentators.

Partially responsible for the confusion in this regard is the interpretation of Israelite wisdom along the lines of the Egyptian concept of *maat*. Although a concern for order was fundamental to the mentality of both the Egyptian and the Israelite sage, the description of that "order" was quite distinct in the two societies. For the Israelite, it was a personal process that remained, in the last analysis, mysterious. For the Egyptian, order was fundamentally a static, impersonal, yet teachable reality. Murphy explains the Egyptian concept this way: "Not only is man to live in harmony with *maat* [the divine order in nature and history], but his very action creates and sustains this divine order in the world."[32]

To the Westerner, *maat* is an illusive word. Having social, ethical, and cosmological dimensions, it is, as R. N. Whybray suggests, "such an all-embracing concept that its translation has often proved difficult. . . . One speaks *maat*, does *maat*, and follows *maat*."[33] To the Egyptian, *maat* is timeless and universal.

---

29. Johnston, " 'Confessions of a Workaholic': A Reappraisal of Qoheleth," p. 27.

30. Von Rad, *Wisdom in Israel*, p. 314.

31. Von Rad, *Wisdom in Israel*, p. 308.

32. Murphy, "Assumptions and Problems in Old Testament Wisdom Research," *Catholic Biblical Quarterly* 29 (1967): 27.

33. Whybray, *Wisdom in Proverbs* (London: SCM Press, 1965), p. 55. The best description of *maat* in the Egyptian sources themselves is found in *Ptah-hotep*.

Though it has a religious thrust, it is not to be simply equated with, nor ultimately based in, the gods. As Henri Frankfort states, "All the gods functioned within the established order; they all lived by *maat*."[34]

One might expect that the Egyptian gods would have brought a personal dimension into this otherwise impersonal ordering of life and cosmos. But as the gods were themselves immanent in nature, they "remain[ed] aloof," Frankfort says. "Their relationship to man [was] indirect."[35] Never directly commanding, the gods instead operated in and through the phenomena, revealing *maat* to the careful observer. For the Egyptian, the proper ordering of life was not mysterious, hostile, or basically problematic. Rather, to quote Frankfort once again, "the Egyptians were evidently convinced that the good life could be taught. Such a conviction betrays a surprising confidence in the efficacy of man's understanding."[36]

The Israelite sage believed that the world is the creation of Yahweh and his ongoing arena. Both nature and history (the Israelite would have felt uncomfortable with this distinction) are controlled by his sovereign hand and ordered by him. The world, therefore, is not static, but a process, an activity of God himself. And God is not under or subject to the divine order, but institutor and controller of it.

In light of this differing orientation, one should not be surprised to see that in Israelite wisdom literature, wisdom comes to man not as a thing but as a person who calls (Prov. 8; Sir. 24). Furthermore, the divine order is not something discernable to all who are silent, but something based on Yahweh and only partially revealed by him to those who are faithful (Prov. 16:9; 25:2). One should not think it strange that wisdom is portrayed as coming from the mouth of the Lord and being given to the upright who are "in his confidence," his intimate circle (Prov. 2:6; 3:32). Nor should one be surprised that in Proverbs 30, Agur is fearful not of destroying the harmonious integration of the existing, impersonal order by being too rich or too poor, but of "denying" Yahweh, whom he calls "my God" (Prov. 30:7-9). Such a personalism is not a part of the Egyptian's understanding of the

---

34. Frankfort, *Ancient Egyptian Religion* (New York: Harper & Row, Harper Torchbooks, 1948), p. 77.

35. Frankfort, *Ancient Egyptian Religion*, p. 81.

36. Frankfort, *Ancient Egyptian Religion*, p. 60.

divine order any more than is the inscrutability or dynamism of Israel's divinely controlled order.

The understanding of order that grew out of Israelite wisdom, at once both personal and partial, avoided all notions of human "reason" that might stress fixity, power, or control. Solomon is our paradigm of the wise man in this regard. Writes von Rad, "A wise and understanding mind, a 'listening' mind—that was the content of Solomon's royal request (1 Kings 3:9). What he . . . wished for himself was not the authoritative reason which reigns supreme over dead natural matter, the reason of modern consciousness, but an 'understanding' reason, a feeling for the truth which emanates from the world and addresses man."[37] Such a receptive posture toward order in human life should not be confused with passivity. For us, order is technically determined; for the ancient sage, it was attained only within mutual trust.

Israel, von Rad says, "believed man to stand in a quite specific, highly dynamic, existential relationship with his environment."[38] Not only is the environment an object of our search for knowledge, but we are as well the object of its divinely appointed favor. Listen, for example, to the way Eliphaz uses traditional wisdom to try to influence Job:

Behold, happy is the man whom God reproves. . . .
In famine he will redeem you from death. . . .
At destruction and famine you shall laugh,
    and shall not fear the beasts of the earth.
For you shall be in league with the stones of the field,
    and the beasts of the field shall be at peace with you. . . .
You shall come to your grave in ripe old age,
    as a shock of grain comes up to the threshing floor in its
    season.
Lo, this we have searched out; it is true.
    Hear, and know it for your good.

(JOB 5:17, 20, 22-23, 26-27)

And hear the writer of Proverbs 16:7:

When a man's ways please the Lord,
    he makes even his enemies to be at peace with him.

---

37. Von Rad, *Wisdom in Israel*, pp. 296-97.
38. Von Rad, *Wisdom in Israel*, p. 301.

Anyone who fails to understand the reciprocity of man and woman with their environment will fail to comprehend wisdom literature's contribution to an environmental ethic.

CONCLUSION

What can we conclude from this overview of wisdom literature? What does its focus upon creation, its rootage in experience, and its concern for order teach the person who would seek to develop a biblical environmental ethic? The following propositions summarize the foregoing discussion and offer ongoing perspective:

1. Life's richness cannot be reduced to cold calculation or to a series of prescriptions. Poetic form might well allow fuller relationships and meanings to come to light than does analytical description. We must realize that form and content go together.

2. The world exists solely because of the continuous care of its Creator and Sustainer. God himself has primary responsibility for creation; humankind is only the vicegerent.

3. Creation does not exist simply for the sake of humankind. It has its own independent value. For this reason, dominion must never be confused with exploitation.

4. Although sin and exploitation are all too evident, an environmental perspective must be built on what should be rather than on what is. The intention of creation is our rightful focus.

5 Creation will reveal its truth to those receptive to it. God's will need not be revealed only through vision or oracle; it can be discerned from observation of life itself.

6. In considering creation, precedence should be given to the concrete and specific rather than to abstract calculation. Experience, not theory, should determine appropriate action.

7. A focus on experience precludes dogmatism and invites continued observation and input. Every judgment is open to correction.

8. Teaching concerning experience is more appropriately seen as advice than as authoritative command. It is always discussable. There needs to be present an openness, a liberality of viewpoint.

9. God is not to be identified with any particular theory or ideology. Immanent in his creation, he is free to respond as he chooses.

10. Wisdom has more to do with observing orderliness than with imposing order. The outworking of creation is controlled by God and revealed only partially to those who are receptive to it.

New Testament Foundations
for
Understanding the Creation

Paulos Mar Gregorios

Recently I was present at a special function at our presidential palace. Zail Singh, the president of India, bestowed a privately endowed honor on one of our most creative friends of nature: Sunderlal Bahuguna. Bahuguna is well known and written about, both in India and abroad. He initiated the Chipko movement, which has been an important factor in awakening Indians to the environmental question, particularly the importance of conserving the forest trees in the Himalayan region.

The mindless and tragic decimation of the Himalayan forests was the result of the government's thoughtless felling of trees in that region. It resulted in heavy soil erosion, desertification, and climate change. After trying many ways of stopping the government, Bahuguna finally launched the "Embrace [chipko] the Trees" movement. He trained the village people to go and embrace a tree as the government workers came to cut it down. The people understood Bahuguna's goal and took on the concerns of the movement with enthusiasm. The highest government officials had to make major decisions to reduce the cutting

Paulos Mar Gregorios *is Metropolitan of Delhi in the Indian Orthodox Church and an outstanding theological thinker. He is also one of the presidents of the World Council of Churches, and chaired the WCC Conference on Faith, Science, and the Future (at M.I.T. in 1979). He is the author of several books, including* The Human Presence: An Orthodox View of Nature *(World Council of Churches, 1978), in which he discusses environmental issues from an Orthodox perspective.*

Unless otherwise noted, the biblical citations in this essay are the author's own translations.

of trees, decisions that would have been politically impossible without the Chipko movement.

Bahuguna is a simple Gandhian. At this function in his honor he said publicly that he was ill at ease on the green lawns of the presidential palace; he wanted to be back among the forest trees and the mountain people. He accepted the award bestowed on him very reluctantly, but expressed happiness that in the process the movement was being recognized.

In his acceptance speech, Bahuguna presented three principles for the environmental movement (which I translate below) that have stayed in my mind:

1. Nature is to be worshiped, not exploited.
2. One who takes less from nature and society should receive greater respect than one who takes more.
3. There is a world inside a person that is richer and more worthy of cultivation than the outside world.

Bahuguna is a Hindu; I am a Christian. As such I must reflect on these principles further rather than accept them at face value. And it is in this context that I seek, trusting in the grace of God and in the power of the Holy Spirit, to examine three passages from the New Testament in order to frame my own principles for the environmental movement. In what follows I will offer my own translation of each of these passages and then discuss the three basic ecological principles I extrapolate from them.

THE THREE PRINCIPLES

I

For I regard the troubles that befall us in this present time as trivial when compared with the magnificent goodness of God that is to be manifested in us. For the created order awaits, with eager longing, with neck outstretched, the full manifestation of the children of God. The futility or emptiness to which the created order is now subject is not something intrinsic to it. The Creator made the creation contingent, in his ordering, upon hope; for the creation itself has something to look forward to—namely, to be freed from its present enslavement to disintegration. The creation itself is to share in the freedom, in the glorious and undying goodness, of the children of God. For we know how the whole creation up till now has been groaning together in agony, in a common pain. And not just the nonhuman created order—even we ourselves, as Christians, who have received the advance gift of the Holy Spirit, are now groaning within ourselves, for we are also waiting—waiting for the transformation of our bodies and for the full experiencing of our adoption as God's children. For it is by that waiting with hope that we are being saved today. We do not hope for something which we already see. Once one sees something, there is no point in continuing to hope to see it. What we hope for is what we have not yet seen; we await its manifestation with patient endurance.

(*ROM. 8:18-25*)

First Principle: Human redemption can be understood only as an integral part of the redemption of the whole creation.

For a long time now we have been conditioned to understand the redemption in Christ primarily—and too often exclusively—in terms of personal salvation. A basic requirement for a healthy Christian approach to the human environment seems to be a shift of gears in this regard.

What is a "person" whose salvation Christ effects? A person exists only in relation—in relation to other human persons (his/her father and mother, to begin with) and to nonhuman realities (light, air, water, food, etc.). It is not possible for a person to come to be or to grow without relation to other persons and things. The earth and the sun as well as other people are an essential part of our existence. Without them we cannot exist.

Both the Pauline and the Johannine witnesses in the New Testament strongly affirm this redemption of the whole creation—cosmic redemption, if you like, or the participation of all creation in the liberation of humanity from the bondage to sin and death. This strongly contradicts the Gnostic-Hellenic-Hindu notion that is most characteristically expressed by Plotinus, the so-called founder of Neoplatonism in the third century:

> No, if body is the cause of Evil, then there is no escape; the cause of Evil is Matter.
>
> (*ENNEADS 1:8:8*)

> Thus, it is quite correct to say at once that Matter is without Quality (in itself) and that it is evil; it is evil not in the sense of having Quality, but precisely, in not having it.
>
> (*ENNEADS 1:8:10*)

In this tradition the body is the source of bondage and evil. Unfortunately, this tradition is also very strong among Christians, who—like Hellenists, Hindus, and Neoplatonists—believe that the soul alone is to be saved, and that the body and other material objects, whether living or nonliving, do not participate in or benefit from the redemption in Christ.

This Gnostic influence in Christianity is what has pervaded our understanding of the Old and the New Testament. Why do we magnify the prophetic and underplay the priestly? We prefer the prophetic because it fits better with our gnostic temperament, which despises the material and the corporate, the sacrificial and the ritual, and prefers to focus on the individual soul and the prophetic word. I will come back to this point later, but here we only need affirm what Saint Paul and Saint John so strongly affirm, contrary to the Gnostic-Hellenic-Hindu tradition, and in the true spirit of the Old Testament: that the whole creation—not just a few human souls—has been redeemed and reconciled in Christ.

Human beings have existed and do exist only as integral parts of a system that includes sources of sustenance—meat, grains, and vegetables—as well as sun and earth, light and water, air and fire. To make a false distinction between "nature" and history, to limit the presence and action of God to history, to deny God's action in "nature"—these cannot be regarded as Christian.

"Nature" in the way in which we use it is not a biblical notion. "Nature" (*physis* in Greek) in the sense of nonhuman self-existent reality does not occur in the Old or the New Testament; it is a concept alien to the biblical world. Insofar as the word "nature" refers to something as it exists by itself, it is contrary to the Johannine affirmation that not a thing came into being without Christ the Logos. If the Old Testament uses the word "nature," it is only in the Book of Maccabees, and there it puts the word in the mouth of a Greek (Antiochus) rather than of a Hebrew.

In fact, there is no Hebrew word for nature. Hebrew uses "creating" (*bara'*) as a verb, but it seldom uses *beriah*, a feminine noun, to refer to the whole creation. It does not make an entity out of the creation, though it recognizes the act that produces and sustains the creation. The Old Testament may make all the trees of the wood rejoice (Ps. 96:12) and ask the trees and animals to praise the Lord (Ps. 148), but it does not speak about "nature" or "the creation" as an entity representing the whole created order.

The New Testament also does not speak of "nature" as the ensemble of created entities. If it uses the word "nature" (in expressions like *physis, physikos, kata physin*), it is to distinguish between natural and unnatural or natural and artificial (see Rom. 1:26, 27; 2:27; 11:21, 24), or to speak about what is spontaneous or connatural. It can speak of our being partakers of the divine nature (in 2 Pet. 1:4, *theias koinōnoi physeōs* literally means "sharers in the nature of the Godhead"), but not of any nature existing independently of God.

Neither is the noun "history" a common biblical notion. Certainly the Bible does not know a God who acts in "history" but does not act in "nature"; it does not distinguish nature from history, as we do. A *historia* is a carefully researched narrative of a series of events, not a realm of exclusively human or divine action unrelated to nature. The noun *historia* does not occur in the Hebrew or Greek Scriptures. The verb *historeo* occurs once (in Gal. 1:18), but it is used to mean "visit."

We have seriously distorted the biblical perspective on redemption by introducing alien categories like "nature" and "history" into it, and by understanding redemption only in terms of souls and persons. In reacting against the exclusive emphasis on personal salvation, Liberalism and neo-orthodoxy fell into the trap of false categories, claiming that God acts in history but not in nature, and that history rather than nature is the realm of God's revelation. These emphases can be traced to a Gnostic bias that detests nature and sacrament as material, but can see history and word as somehow nonmaterial and (therefore?) spiritual.

A new understanding of the redemption in Jesus Christ will then have to take into account at least the following: (a) personal and corporate salvation; (b) spiritual reality and material reality in the creation and in the Incarnation; (c) the created order as the object and field of the redeeming order; and (d) the human person as integrally related to the whole cosmos. When we keep these relationships in mind, we will have a picture of our own faith that will facilitate a more respectful approach not to "nature" but to the created order as a whole. The continuity between the order of creation and the order of redemption, rather than their distinction and difference, should be the focus of our interest. Humanity is redeemed *with* the created order, not *from* it.

II

He, Christ, the Beloved Son, is the manifest presence (icon) of the unmanifest God. He is the Elder Brother of all things created, for it was by him and in him that all things were created, whether here on earth in the sensible world or in the world beyond the horizon of your senses which we call heaven, even institutions like royal thrones, seats of lords and rulers—all forms of authority. All things were created through him, by him, in him. But he himself is before all things; in him they consist and subsist; he is the head of the body, the Church. He is the New Beginning, the Firstborn from the dead; thus he becomes in all respects pre-eminent. For it was (God's) good pleasure that in Christ all fullness should dwell; it is through him and in him that all things are to be reconciled and reharmonized. For he has removed the contradiction and made peace by his own blood. So all things in the visible earth and in the invisible heaven should dwell together in him.

That includes you, who were once alienated, enemies in your own minds to

God's purposes, immersed in evil actions; but now you are bodily reconciled in his fleshly body which has tasted death. Christ intends to present you—holy, spotless, and blameless—in God's presence, if you remain firm in the faith, rooted and grounded in him, unswerving from the hope of the good news you have heard, the good news declared not only to men and women on earth, but to all created beings under heaven. It is this gospel that I, Paul, have also been called to serve.

(COL. 1:15-23)

Second Principle: Christ himself should be seen in his three principal relationships: (1) to members incorporated into his body, (2) to the human race, and (3) to the other than human orders of created existence in a many-planed universe. Each of these is related to the other.

A Christology based on this principle will not conceive of a Christ as somehow other than the created order. Today much of Christology sees Christ as being separate from the world, from culture, and so forth; we try to affirm the Lordship of Christ *over* world and culture by conceiving even the incarnate Christ as somehow totally distinct from the created order. We then think of him as Lord of the world, Lord of the church, and so on. In the more individualistic versions of Christology-soteriology, some make him "sole mediator" between the person and God. This perception involves three realities: God, Christ, and the individual. God is there, the individual is here, and Christ stands in between. And the world and the church are fourth and fifth realities.

This kind of disjunctive thinking has to give way to an integral and participative way of understanding Christ. Jesus Christ is not an abstract or "purely spiritual" entity. He is incarnate. He took a material body, becoming part of the created order while remaining unchanged as one of the three persons in the Trinity who is Creator. He is one of us. He is fully consubstantial with us.

As Christians we are united with him in an especially intimate way. By baptism and by faith, he has incorporated us as members of his body. By participation in his body and blood, we grow to be integral parts of him. Once he had a human body like ours. In fact, he still does—though it has already been transformed and resurrected and is therefore no longer subject to the ordinary laws of our physics, which govern only mortal bodies and material objects. But he has chosen to have a larger body, partly in heaven (i.e., beyond the horizon of our senses) and partly here on earth. We belong to that body as a whole, but particularly to the earthly part of it. Christ is always with us, the members of his body, particularly as he continues to fulfill his ministry as High Priest of creation and as Prophet and Servant to the world.

Christ incarnate is a human being, consubstantial with all other human beings. He did not become simply an individual human person or a Christian. He became *humankind*—male and female. He assumed the whole of human nature, and now there is no humanity other than the one which Christ took on—our humanity, in which all human beings participate, whether or not they believe in Christ, whether or not they recognize the nature of their humanity. This aspect of the Redeemer's relationship to the whole of humanity, independent of human faith, is seldom fully recognized by Christians and its implications worked out. No human beings are alien to Christ, whether they be Hindu, Muslim, Communist, or Buddhist. They share in Christ's humanity in ways that we have to spell out elsewhere. They are not members of the body of Christ, but they are not unrelated to Christ.

Christ the Incarnate One assumed flesh—organic, human flesh; he was nurtured by air and water, vegetables and meat, like the rest of us. He took matter into himself, so matter is not alien to him now. His body is a *material* body—transformed, of course, but transformed *matter*. Thus he shares his being with the whole created order: animals and birds, snakes and worms, flowers and seeds. All parts of creation are now reconciled to Christ. And the created order is to be set free and to share in the glorious freedom of the children of God. Sun and moon, planets and stars, pulsars and black holes—as well as the planet earth—are to participate in that final consummation of the redemption.

The risen Christ is thus active, by the Spirit, in all three realms: in the church, in the whole of humanity, and in the cosmos. Each of these relationships is fundamentally different, but all are real and meaningful to Christ the Incarnate One.

Our theology's weakness has been its failure to recognize the wider scope of the redemption beyond the "individual soul" or the person. Liberalism still spiritualizes the incarnate Christ by confining his actions to so-called history, as if that were a realm in which "nature" and the material elements of creation were not present. We must move beyond personal salvation to declare and teach the three basic dimensions of the redemption.

III

At the source-spring of all, the Logos is and was. The Logos is God's vis-à-vis, and the Logos is God. It is this Logos that in the beginning was face to face with God. It is through the Logos that all existing things have come to exist. Without him not a single thing could have come into being. In him was also life. Life is light in human beings. The light shines in the midst of the darkness, and the darkness has not comprehended or overcome the light.

(JOHN 1:1-5)

Third Principle: Christ and the Holy Spirit are related to the whole created order in three ways: by creating it, by redeeming it, and by finally fulfilling it in the last great consummation.

There is no need to elaborate these points. The act of creation is a corporate act of the three persons of the Trinity. God's relation to plants and trees, to air and water did not begin with the redemption in the incarnate Christ. Not a single thing exists that did not come into being without Christ and the Holy Spirit, including the primeval water over which the Spirit was hovering at the time of creation (Gen. 1:2). Neither art nor literature, neither mountain nor river, neither flower nor field came into existence without Christ and the Holy Spirit. They exist now because they are sustained by God. The creative energy of God is the true being of all that is; matter is that spirit or energy in physical form. Therefore, we should regard our human environment as the energy of God in a form that is accessible to our senses.

We have already discussed the relationship of the human environment, of the whole cosmos, to the redemption. It is a redeemed cosmos that we meet in our environment, and as such it is worthy of respect.

It is the final *apokatastasis*, the fulfillment at the end, that still needs to be stressed. The consummation, which Paul calls *anakephalaiōsis*, means adding up everything (Eph. 1:10)—that is, the consummation of the whole created order in Christ. Take the three numbers 5, 7, and 14. When one adds them up, one gets 26. At first it may not be obvious that the three smaller numbers are contained in the larger number, but they are there; they are not lost. Analogous to this is the process in the final *apokatastasis*, about which Peter preached in Solomon's Portico in Jerusalem. There he talked about "Christ Jesus, whom the unseen realm must keep until the times of the final restitution of all things, about which God spoke through the mouths of his holy ones the prophets from ages ago" (Acts 3:21; my translation).

The Christian understanding of the status of the world, of

all life and of inorganic matter, is determined by these three factors:

Q. How did they come to be, and how are they sustained?
A. By creation.

Q. How does the Incarnation of Jesus Christ affect them?
A. They share in the destined freedom of the children of God.

Q. What is their final destiny?
A. To be incorporated, through transformation, in the new order that fully emerges only at the end, in the final recapitulation.

The whole created order comes from God the Holy Trinity, is redeemed by the incarnate Christ, and will be brought to fulfillment after transformation by the same Christ and by the Holy Spirit, the perfecter of all.

REFUTING BAHUGUNA

Now that we have explored these three basic Christian principles, we are in a position to look again at Sunderlal Bahuguna's three principles.

As for his first principle, Christians cannot say that nature is to be *worshiped* and not exploited. Christians would say that the created order (not nature) is to be *respected* as the order that has given birth to us, sustains us, and will still be the framework for our existence when the whole process of creation-redemption has been consummated. We respect the created order both because it comes from God and is sustained by him, and because it is the matrix of our origin, growth, and fulfillment as human beings. But we do not worship the creation; worship is reserved for the Creator. We have to *tend* the creation, use it for our own sustenance and flourishing, but we also have to respect it in itself as a manifestation of God's creative energy and cooperate with God in bringing out the full splendor of the created order as reflecting the glory of the Creator.

Bahuguna's second principle—that one who takes less from nature is to be more honored than one who takes more—is also dubious from a Christian perspective. Simplicity of life is a high value, but enforced poverty is not. And the poor are to be respected not because they take less from nature but because they are the friends of God and the victims of injustice. Christians can choose from two life-styles: the simple life à la John the Baptist, who lived on locusts and wild honey in the desert, and the fuller life of our Lord, who prayed all night and worked all day, but who also ate and drank with others. Neither of these life-styles would, however, justify the mindless affluence of our consumer society. To impose austerity on a society may be unwise, but it is even more unwise to impose affluence on a nation through hidden persuasion, and to make some people more affluent than others. In taking what is given by "nature," we should be careful to give back to "nature" what it needs to maintain its own integrity and to supply the needs of the future.

Bahuguna's third principle—that the individual's inner life is more worthy of development than the outside world—is also wrongheaded. Christians need not despise or reject the outer world in order to develop the inner world. And we should not think of the inner world as an individual realm. Rather, we should think of it as the unseen, the heavenly, that which lies *beyond* our senses. It is a different perception, one that Paul talks about when he says, "If then you have co-risen with Christ, seek the higher things, where Christ now is enthroned at the right hand of God. Meditate on and will the heavenly realities, not the earthly ones" (Col. 3:1-2; my translation). We should not speak of the inner world but of the final fulfillment that is already present in the realm beyond our senses, and that now moves our world as its norm and goal. Even when we are thinking about the environment or socio-economic and political life—*ta anō phroneite*. We should focus our minds and wills on the higher realities (not the inner), which must be manifested in the earthly realities—now partially, but in the end, fully.

The Church's Role
in Healing the Earth

MARY EVELYN JEGEN

To consider the church's role in healing the earth, we need to
have clearly in mind a concept of the church. No single concept,
description, or definition of the church is adequate to the reality,
and this is to our advantage for a number of reasons, not the least
of which is that it should keep us from distorting the richness of
the church by absolutizing any one concept. I propose three rich
concepts of the church that will help us consider the role of the
church in healing the earth: the church as a community of disciples, the church as mother, and the church as teacher.

THE CHURCH AS A COMMUNITY OF DISCIPLES

The church should be viewed as a community of disciples because a community of disciples is precisely what Jesus founded.
A disciple is not merely a pupil or even a student, someone bent
on mastering a body of knowledge. Rather, a disciple is one who
learns by way of sharing life with a master until the way of life and

*MARY EVELYN JEGEN, S.N.D., holds an M.A. in religious studies from Mun-
delein College and a Ph.D. in history from St. Louis University. She is Vice
President of Pax Christe International, and was formerly National Coordinator
of Pax Christe USA. She teaches in the theology departments of Creighton
University and Mundelein College, and gives retreats, workshops, and lectures
in the United States and Europe. She has written widely on peace and justice
topics. Her most recent book is* How You Can Be a Peacemaker *(Liquori
Publications, 1985).*

*Unless otherwise noted, the biblical citations in this essay are taken from the
Jerusalem Bible, copyright © 1966, 1967 and 1968 by Darton, Longman & Todd
Ltd. and Doubleday & Company, Inc.*

the attitudes, habits, skills, and traditions of the master become part of the disciple's own life.

Jesus himself was a disciple of God, whom he came to know by the familiar term "Abba," which was a radical departure from the prevailing custom of calling God "Creator" and "Lord."[1] "Abba" does not deny or exclude the idea of God as Creator and Lord, but it appropriates this into a new experience—that of God as a source as intimate as, and even more intimate than, one's own biological father. Our parents really live on in us. When I look down at my hands, I sometimes remember that the tissue that has grown organically all these years began as the union of elements from my parents' bodies. Parents do live in their children.

Jesus was the disciple of Abba, and he was tutored in this discipleship by also being a disciple of Mary in his childhood. The Gospel accounts show her among Jesus' disciples later in his public life, so their relationship extended throughout his life in an intimate and privileged way. It is unmistakeable from the Gospel accounts that this woman who treasured her experience (pondering it in her heart, as Luke says) passed on this habit to her son. He was an exquisitely attentive person, a contemplative person who delighted in the beauties of nature. He did more than delight—he cared. He had his own disciples gather the leftovers from the meal for the five thousand; he admired good craftsmanship; he knew the ways of the shepherd and the vinedresser. His contemplative and inventive gifts were brought together in the act of greatest daring and clarity when he took bread into his hands, blessed it, and broke it, and took a cup of wine and blessed it, and gave both to his disciples, saying that the bread and the wine were his own body and blood. They were instructed to repeat the ritual in his memory.

In trying to come to terms with the mystery of the relationship between the spiritual and the material, between the immanent and the transcendent, in trying to find ways of healing the earth, we cannot do better than to begin and end our search in the Gospel.

One of the things that most strikes me about considering the church as a community of disciples is that it protects us against making a false separation between people and other created

---

1. See Joachim Jeremias, *New Testament Theology: The Proclamation of Jesus* (New York: Scribner's, 1971), pp. 59-61; and Avery Dulles, S.J., *A Church to Believe In: Discipleship and the Dynamics of Freedom* (New York: Crossroad, 1982), pp. 1-18.

goods while at the same time it teaches us to give the appropriate place to humankind in the order of creation. As disciples of Jesus, we depend for our salvation precisely upon how we relate to people and to the goods of the earth. The norm for using goods (and therefore the earth that is their source) is to use them to meet the needs of those in whom God dwells, with whom God identifies. "Come, you whom my Father has blessed. . . . For I was hungry and you gave me food" (Matt. 25:34-35).

As long as we try to develop a norm for distribution of the earth's resources according to any economic system that sees the goods of creation primarily as commodities to be owned, we will never find a norm that is equitable or that respects the earth itself. On the other hand, when we look first at people and their inherent claim to integral human development—and, therefore, to their needs—we are brought to a posture of reverence and care. Gandhi showed that he understood this more deeply than many professed Christians when he made the acute observation that there is enough for each person's need but not enough for each person's greed. With regard to possessions, he said that a person's goal should be to see how much he/she can do without. Whatever persons have beyond their needs, he declared, is stolen from the poor.

Viewing the church as a community of disciples suggests that one important role for the church is to help us return to our senses. What do I mean by that? The Christian church is a consequence of the most daring of all beliefs: that God became incarnate in the person of Jesus Christ. This is not the place to examine different theological explanations of the Incarnation—that is, to attempt to explain what it means that this man, Jesus, is God, or how his divine and human natures are united in a single person. In accepting this doctrine of our faith, we can draw—must draw—two conclusions that are germane to our topic. One is that the intimacy of the relationship between divinity and the material creation, between God and the world, is beyond our wildest dreams. Who of us, if we had not been given the gift of faith, would propose a theological hypothesis that someday God might save the world by assuming the nature of a human being, by becoming a specific person with a body, a mind, and emotions like ours?

By reason of this Incarnation of the Second Person of the Trinity, all creation is made holy. The early fathers liked to say that all the waters of the earth had been sanctified by Jesus' baptism in the Jordan. This penetrating view of matter can be extended to all creation. An Irish poet, Joseph Mary Plunkett, expressed it thus in "I See His Blood upon the Rose":

> I see His blood upon the rose
> And in the stars the glory of His eyes;
> His body gleams amid eternal snows,
> His tears fall from the skies.

> I see His face in every flower;
> The thunder and the singing of the birds
> Are but His voice—and carven by His power
> Rocks are His written words.

> All pathways by His feet are worn,
> His strong heart stirs the everbeating sea,
> His crown of thorns is twined with every thorn,
> His cross is every tree.

Christianity calls us to return to our senses and to see all created things as sharing in the splendor of the Incarnation. In the thirteenth century, the theologian Thomas Aquinas taught that God is in all things by his essence, presence, and power. In the sixteenth century the Spanish mystic Ignatius of Loyola taught his companions to contemplate God toiling for them in the works of created nature.

The return to the senses does not come easily to us. We are heirs not only to a Judeo-Christian worldview but also to that of the Greeks. As a result of the latter, we have a long tradition of seeing the soul as somehow imprisoned in the body, a body that is seen as a kind of house or dwelling place for what is really important: the immaterial soul. There is a related stream in our tradition that sees the body as an obstacle to genuine spiritual life, as something to be despised. It is not useful to reject completely the Greek philosophical view of life, because it has some precious elements of truth and real value. However, for our purposes it is very important to affirm strongly the goodness and holiness and very real importance of everything material if we are to come to some kind of wisdom about the healing of the earth.

Perhaps it is here that we should examine more closely the notion of healing. Healing refers first to bodily reality, and only by extension to what is immaterial. While we can talk about healing a relationship, for example, we speak this way only from our direct experience of bodily healing. Healing takes place only after an illness or a wound. While illnesses and wounds are not identical, they both result in damage to a complex living organism. Thus we can talk of wounded animals but not of a wounded chair or table—only a broken one. Wounds are painful and also threatening because they remind us of our mortality. If they are serious and are left unattended, and if they do not heal, they will bring a living organism to death.

The verb "to heal" is related to the Indo-European root *Kailo*, which means whole, uninjured. It is also related to Old English *halig*, meaning holy, sacred, and to *hailagon*, which means to consecrate, to hallow.

This observation brings us to one of the most mysterious passages of the New Testament, one that brings us closer to the appropriate way of the church in the healing of the earth. In the First Letter of Peter, a letter that scholars tell us was probably used as an early baptismal instruction, we read the following:

> Christ suffered for you and left an example for you to follow the way he took. He had not done anything wrong, and there had been no perjury in his mouth. He was insulted and did not retaliate with insults; when he was tortured he made no threats but he put his trust in the righteous judge. He was bearing our faults in his own body on the cross, so that we might die to our faults and live for holiness; through his wounds you have been healed. You had gone astray like sheep but now you have come back to the shepherd and guardian of your souls.

> *(1 Pet. 2:21-25)*

Here we get some intimation of the way of healing that is proper to the church. It is clear that Christian wisdom does not see healing as something to be achieved by way of diagnosing an ailment or locating a wound and then applying an external remedy at not much cost to the healer beyond skill, attention, and commitment of time. Jesus' way of healing, the way to which the church is called, is by way of taking upon oneself the very weakness and wounds of the sufferer.

The passage quoted, of course, is speaking of us. What does it tell us about healing the earth? I think it tells us first that it is not enough to correct an angle of vision, to see ourselves as participating in the life system of the earth while at the same time in some way standing over against it—not to dominate it but to appropriate it in order that it may share in our glorifying God. This conversion of vision is necessary, but it is not enough. We also need conversion of heart and compassion so that we enter into the suffering of the earth, so that we do not try to escape from it or remedy it from the outside, but rather that in love we take it upon ourselves, into ourselves. In sharing its wounds, we will become participants in the healing of the earth.

Once we accept this, we are, I believe, in a better position to deal with a troubling and central issue that continually faces us as we try to accept the responsibility we have for the condition of the earth. We can feel compassion only for our own kind. We recognize that our ecosystem has a certain wholeness, but at the same time we realize that our being human separates us from that system in a critical way. In coming to understand and accept our responsibility as earthkeepers, we must not fall into the error of blurring the distinction between the different orders of creation. God has crowned us with glory and honor and made us a little lower than the angels (Ps. 8). The same thing cannot be said of dolphins or redwood trees or the oceans and rivers that are part of our earth system. It is precisely in compassion for our own kind that we can be brought into the posture of contemplation that helps us give the appropriate weight to all that we encounter in the experience of living.

In the Christian tradition, a person who is universally recognized as being a most exemplary member of the community of disciples is Francis of Assisi. He has given us one of our most beautiful Christian classics, a gem-like theology of the environment in miniature, in his *Canticle of Brother Sun*. It expresses most beautifully a profound and balanced Christian response to the gift of creation. Perhaps one of the best contributions we could make to the stewardship of the earth would be the frequent incorporation of this beautiful hymn into our worship. In it Francis sings,

Oh, Most High, Almighty, Good Lord God,
to Thee belong praise, glory, honor, and all blessing.

Praised be my Lord God, with all His creatures,
and especially our brother the Sun,
who brings us the day and who brings us the light:
fair is he, and he shines with a very great splendor,
O Lord, he signifies thee to us!

Praised be my Lord for our sister the Moon, and for the stars,
the which He has set clear and lovely in the heavens.

Praised be my Lord for our brother the wind,
and for air and clouds, calms and all weather,
by which Thou upholdest life and all creatures.

Praised be my Lord for our sister water,
who is very serviceable to us, and humble and precious and
    clean.

Praised be my Lord for our brother fire,
through whom Thou givest us light in the darkness;
and he is bright and pleasant and very mighty and strong.

Praised be my Lord for our mother the earth,
the which doth sustain us and keep us,
and bringeth forth divers fruits and flowers of many colors,
and grass.

Praised be my Lord for all those who pardon one another for
love's sake,
and who endure weakness and tribulation.
Blessed are they who peacefully shall endure,
for Thou, O Most High, wilt give them a crown.

Praised be my Lord for our sister, the death of the body,
from which no man escapeth.
Woe to him who dieth in mortal sin.
Blessed are those who die in Thy most holy will,
for the second death shall have no power to do them harm.
Praise ye and bless the Lord, and give thanks to Him,
and serve Him with great humility.

THE CHURCH AS MOTHER

The second model of the church that can help us get in touch with
her healing role is the church as mother. This symbol accents the
nurturing dimension of the church. Mothering by its very nature
is a most intimate and organic relationship. If we grant that it is in
and through the church that we come to our own experience of
God in Christ, we can appreciate the aptness of this symbol,
which protects us from seeing God as somehow outside, operat-
ing from a distance.

This beautiful symbol of church as mother has its roots in
Scripture, in those passages that use feminine and specifically
maternal imagery for Jerusalem, the prototype of the church.
Consider the following:

Rejoice, Jerusalem,
be glad for her, all you who love her!
Rejoice, rejoice for her,
all you who mourned her!

That you may be suckled, filled,
from her consoling breast,
that you may savor with delight
her glorious breasts.

For thus says Yahweh:
Now toward her I send flowing
peace, like a river,
and like a stream in spate
the glory of the nations.

At her breast will her nurslings be carried
and fondled in her lap.
Like a son comforted by his mother
will I comfort you.
(And by Jerusalem you will be comforted.)

(Isa. 66:10-13)

There is an unbroken tradition of seeing the church as mother extending back to the early fathers. Saint Cyprian, for example, speaks of the church's guarding us and keeping us together in her maternal heart. The characteristic quality of our mother the church is caring. It may surprise us to discover that the word "care" includes the notion of anxiety for another, an attention marked by strong emotion. The word "care" comes from an old Germanic root that means to cry out. Thus "care" adds to the notion of contemplation an intense emotional involvement that includes compassion, a capacity for sharing in the suffering of one for whom a mother is responsible as life-bearer and nurturer.

Philosopher Milton Mayeroff has written a beautiful book, *On Caring*, in which he shows that through caring a person "lives the meaning of his own life" and finds his proper relationship with others and with things. Says Mayeroff, in a sentence that I consider one of the wisest I have ever read, "In the sense in which a man can ever be said to be at home in the world, he is at home not through dominating, or explaining, or appreciating, but through caring and being cared for."[2] While Mayeroff does not correlate caring with the feminine aspects of personhood, I suggest that caring relates very aptly to the concept of the church as mother.

Ever since I read an account of it in the newspaper, I have been intrigued by an incident that occurred during the May 1984 visit of Pope John Paul II to the Supreme Patriarch of the Buddhists of Thailand. It can help explain the relationship of contemplation and caring and at the same time bring us to a better understanding of contemplation directed toward people. The ac-

---

2. Mayeroff, *On Caring* (New York: Harper & Row, 1971), p. 2.

count noted that during the pope's thirty-minute social visit, the eighty-six-year-old patriarch sat cross-legged on a cushion. During one five-minute period there was absolute silence as the pope and the patriarch exchanged fraternal glances.

I know nothing of this practice beyond what I read in the paper, but from the story I am presuming that exchanging fraternal glances is a customary ritual and that it is governed by protocol. I imagine that the pope had to practice fraternal glancing in advance, since we Westerners are not trained to spend five minutes in absolute silence during a social encounter—much less to exchange fraternal glances. I began to think of what such a custom might mean if adopted in our own culture.

Imagine, for example, that diplomats were trained to exchange fraternal glances in silence, and that members of Congress were likewise instructed. Suppose that we taught our children the art of looking lovingly, in silence, at their parents and teachers, and that we taught parents and teachers to do the same. Imagine what might happen if in all conflict situations—in marital arguments, in labor-management relations, in city-hall politics, in court battles—we were all trained to look lovingly, and that this was a mutual looking, as in the case of the pope and the patriarch. I wonder how decisions would be affected, how conflicts might be resolved.

Can we, the church, learn from the Buddhist culture a practice that might help us get in touch with our own tradition and wisdom of contemplation? Contemplation can be abused and become an escape from the world and our responsibilities. However, it can also be the indispensable key to healing. Fundamentally, what contemplation involves is the act of paying attention, of directing our powers toward another in an attitude of reverence and receptivity. Contemplation is not mere seeing, and it is the opposite of staring and even of mere gazing. It is at once restful and alert, open to the heightened experience and truth that arises from this act of attending.

Caring contemplation, as I am discussing it, leads—though not necessarily or inevitably—to understanding, to a profound insight into the heart of the matter we are contemplating. Understanding in turn both calls us and enables us to be reasonable, to weigh sides of an issue, to see various facets of a situation or an object of our attention. This kind of reasonableness then calls us to respond, to take appropriate action. Our response will be in proportion to the depth from which it springs. Blessed are we if we are founded in the world of faith, and twice blessed are we if we are grounded in love.[3]

Since 1973 I have been making an effort to deepen my own understanding of the biblical mystery of stewardship, convinced that this mystery can provide us with the foundation for a sound and developmental approach to issues of ecology, social justice, and economic structures—an approach that will not oppress and exploit the poor, who are the majority of the world's population. I still hold these convictions. However, I now believe that our efforts to promote an understanding and practice of stewardship have relied too much—in some cases, almost exclusively—on analysis, an approach that operates on the assumption that if people understand what is right, they will do what is right.

Evidence abounds that this is far from universally true. It is not true when understanding occurs only on the level of cause and effect. For example, people know that smoking causes cancer and continue to smoke; they know that selfishness leads to loneliness and unhappiness, and continue to act selfishly. The list is endless. On the other hand, when people understand on a deeper level—when they resonate, as it were, with a level of truth beyond the scope or attainment of everyday logic—they act on their beliefs. This is the kind of understanding that makes parents commit themselves to lives of unobtrusive service and sacrifice, that drives artists and inventors, that makes some doctors excellent diagnosticians, that led Jesus to lay down his life for his friends, and that has inspired some of his followers as well as other noble people who are not Christian to do the same.

Stewardship has failed where it has been reduced to a reasonable way of managing time, talent, and treasure for the sake of the kingdom as we understand it; where it has not created a moral and religious imperative for rectifying the massive structural injustices that make life short and cruel for millions; where it has not moved people to commit themselves to changing the structures that support injustice. The biblical concept of stewardship will become a powerful idea whose time has come when and only when it springs from a contemplative vision that sees God, people, and the goods of the earth in a creative and dynamic tension in which the way of union with God and people is precisely

---

3. See Bernard Lonergan, *Method in Theology* (New York: Herder & Herder, 1972), p. 242; and *Second Collection* (London: Darton, Longman & Todd, 1974), pp. 161-62.

through the sharing of the goods we hold in trust. The key word here, and the one that is too easily overlooked, is *sharing*.

Most of us still see goods; air, fire, water, the earth and any of its fruits are things to be used and ultimately owned by an individual, a corporation, or the state. Biblical stewardship depends on a contemplative experience that sees relationships in a different way. What is this experience? It is seeing the purpose of created goods, including all the earth, as *sharing*, as *the means of union between and among people*. We, alas, are so conditioned to seeing the purpose of goods as *having* that the assertion that goods are meant precisely to be circulated or shared may strike us as out of touch with reality.

Goods are for sharing; the earth is for sharing. What are the implications of this thesis? Imagine that you hold in your hand a hundred dollars, and that you decide to give it away. When you have given away fifty dollars, you will have less money; when you have given the other fifty away, you will have none. Now imagine yourself making a conscious decision to do something kind, a very particular kind deed. You may decide, for example, to make a point of telling a colleague how happy you are about her recent promotion, or letting a friend know how much you enjoyed her recently published article. By such an action, you have given some kindness and at the same time increased your own. You are a kinder person.

The point is simple: just as we divide material goods by sharing them, we multiply spiritual goods by sharing them. The very purpose of material goods is to act as the mechanism for sharing, the vehicle for enabling us to come into deeper communion with our brothers and sisters. When we see things this way, we do not try to work up our generosity to give things away, but rather we look for ways to share. We do not lose what we share; we simply forge or reinforce the bonds that make us more deeply human. All this is possible only if we develop the habit of care and contemplation, the habit of paying loving attention. "Happy are your eyes because they see" (Matt. 13:16).

THE CHURCH AS TEACHER

As we have seen, the fact that no single concept or description of the church is adequate to her reality is to our advantage, for it keeps us from distorting the richness of the church by absolutizing any one description. We now consider the church as teacher, as tutor and instructor in the faith. She is a teacher in precisely the way she is a mother—in a feminine way, a way that is highly intuitive and affective, that is not prone to think of mind or soul as separate from body. Where a man wants to command and control, a woman wants to establish harmony, to make things go smoothly.

What should the church teach that will help heal the earth? The church has a special responsibility to teach interdependence, the interconnectedness of all things. She has a special responsibility to teach that we are linked together in a limited world, vulnerable to each other's actions and responsible for each other's lives. She has a special credibility in this area, because in her own history she has demonstrated (albeit imperfectly) that interconnectedness in her ability to link people of many different cultures into a single communion. This transnational and transcultural quality of the church witnesses to the hope for a way of relationship based on shared vision, shared values, and a shared understanding of a common human vocation to dwell on the earth as stewards, not as ruthless and rapacious dominators.

From one point of view, it is almost impossible *not* to come to some sense of global interdependence today. We all experience interdependence as a consequence of the industrial and technological revolutions. Schoolchildren know that pollution affects the global environment in the most radical ways and that it threatens to destroy the delicate envelope of air on which all planetary life depends; they know that the life-giving waters of the planet can be made lifeless by industrial wastes dumped into major waterways. Pollution happens without regard for national boundaries. The only way governments can protect the underpinnings of life for their own people is by cooperating with other governments and by exercising self-discipline in their own economic systems.

These easily observable facts of life should be interpreted and taught by the church, in season and out of season, from the horizon of Christian faith. In interdependence, faith recognizes a call to a deeper dedication to the entire human race, a race that we know as the family of God. We need to encourage and affirm all our skilled teachers and artists who can help us grasp the truth that our first identification must be with the entire human family. We need to pledge our first and deepest allegiance to the political reality of the human race as one. The unity of the human family takes priority over any distinction based on national groupings. This does not mean that we reject or abandon our loyalty and our responsibility to our own nation, but that we transcend it, that we appropriate it into the only frame of reference that is adequate to our present situation as human beings.

Loyalty is more than an intellectual conviction. It carries strong emotion of the kind that orders our actions. We need only think of the way we experience loyalty to a child, a spouse, or a family. Loyalty moves us to the most generous and self-sacrificing love and behavior. In our tradition we have many examples of loyalty, among them the many men who have given their lives in war to defend values we hold dear. We also have examples of misdirected loyalty, of loyalty abused. Consider the fierce loyalty of the members of a street gang. The point I am trying to make is that in our effort to rise to our responsibilities as stewards of the earth, we need to attend to more than the skills of argument and persuasion. We need also to tap the deep springs of emotion that drive us. Among them, loyalty is paramount.[4]

For us, the most splendid example of loyalty is that of Jesus as it has come to us in the Gospel accounts of his relationship to his disciples and to his own people. He was loyal to both to the end. At the same time, his was a love that was not narrowly confined to either of these associations. Fidelity to his vision made it possible for his first followers to become missionary, to extend their horizons and the boundaries of their community even to the ends of the earth.

The teaching of the church, though it includes instruction, is much more than that. It involves, as we know, the induction into a way of life, a way of life built on faith. While faith is not inconsistent with reason, it is also not amenable to methods of scientific research and experimentation. Put another way, we who are Christians are acting from a perspective that sees life as much more than a set of problems that we can fully comprehend and, given time, can control. We experience life as both a problem to be solved and a mystery to be lived. Mystery is not comprehended; it is participated in, shared, celebrated. Think of the mystery of a marriage, for example. Partners do not "solve" a marriage; they live it.

The role of the church as a teacher on environmental issues is to help us as its members and others who are directly or indirectly influenced to experience the environment not only—or

---

4. The works of Christian economist Barbara Ward convey well the notion of loyalty discussed here. See, for example, *The Home of Man* (New York: W. W. Norton, 1976), and *Progress for a Small Planet* (New York: W. W. Norton, 1979).

even primarily—as something outside ourselves that we can control. Certainly our response to the environment includes this dimension, and we need all the scientific learning and careful skill and understanding we can achieve in order to know how to handle the environment. But we are faced with such dilemmas that unless we are given a key to interpret our situation as involving more than problems we can solve, we may give up in despair. Indeed, many people have—consciously or not—despaired and given up, and this accounts for the difficulty in arousing public opinion on environmental issues.

Let me give a simple example. We know that many of our serious and mammoth environmental problems—problems that almost immediately turn out to be human tragedies—spring from well-intended interventions in the environment. For example, the desertification of the widening belt around the equator in Africa is the consequence of the overgrazing of cattle—overgrazing that is the result of an effort to improve the lot of the people who live there. Similarly, flooding in Bangladesh is directly related to deforestation in the Himalayas caused by rampant woodcutting for much-needed fuel.

Do we have any ways, any indices for measuring or forecasting the unintended side effects of our actions on the environment, the collateral damage that results from our best efforts to improve the lot of others? By this time, with all the surveys we have taken and all the knowledge we have acquired of the troubled state of our planet, it should be clear to us that there is a missing piece, that we must look elsewhere than to science, economics, and politics for a key to our problem. Where can we find such a key?

Here is where the faith we hold and the Gospel we believe can provide us with a key or clue to our situation. We must look first not to analysis but to vision and attitude. At the same time, we need to have at our disposal something much more useful than principles that remain on a level so far removed from reality that they do not offer adequate guidance. We need tools of interpretation that are midway between principles and concrete, specific policies.

I propose that we have available such a set of middle-range guidelines to help us on the environmental issues, and that these principles spring directly from a Gospel vision of the meaning of the human person and the world. These middle-range guidelines will give us directions for participating in the mystery of life while enhancing our environment rather than inflicting damage on it.

The guidelines I will explain come from the theory of integral development by Louis Lebret, the French Dominican pioneer of development economics who died in the late 1960s.[5] According to Lebret, the first question that must be asked of any economic action ("economic" in this context indicating a plan of management) is, How does the production, distribution, and consumption of a resource meet a human need? The crucial point here is that the person in community is central to every economic question. One never asks about production simply in terms of profit and loss. It is necessary to go further because the notion of need is too broad to be useful of itself. Lebret distinguished three kinds of needs, and it is here that he made part of his great contribution.

First are subsistence needs, those things we must have in order to maintain life so that it is capable of development: food, clothing, shelter, and also health care and education. (We could add that a stable government is likewise a subsistence need.) Second are those needs related to comfort and facilities. These are needs that are clearly different from subsistence needs but yet are true needs—for example, transportation, labor-saving devices, art, and the like. It is possible to put a price tag on the goods that supply these needs because they are as measurable as the goods of subsistence. At times they may be luxuries, but most often they are not. Third are our needs for transcendence, real though intangible claims that are inherent because we are human beings open to God, made in God's very image. The goods that satisfy our transcendence needs cannot be measured or priced, but they are no less real. They include religion and friendship. Without these goods our lives would be little different from those of the animals with which we have so much in common.

Recognizing these different but related needs, Lebret outlined the basic guidelines for a development policy. A society, he said, should aim to provide subsistence goods for everyone as a human right, *without violating transcendence needs*. Then, to the extent to which it is capable, society should work to satisfy the second category of needs.

Examined against this theory, both the prevailing capitalist system and the Marxist-Communist economic system are found wanting, but for different reasons. Capitalism, in both its unmodified and its modified forms, relies on the drive for growth,

---

5. An excellent treatment of Lebret's development theory is found in Denis Goulet, *The New Moral Order: Development Ethics and Liberation Theology* (Maryknoll, N.Y.: Orbis Books, 1974), pp. 23-49.

and growth in turn depends on an expanding market that responds to effective demand. For reasons that are patent, this demand arises from those who want so-called enhancement goods because they have satisfied their needs for subsistence goods. In fact, this system depends on feeding greed, and it does this at the expense of those who need subsistence goods but cannot get into the market because they do not have the money or credit to enter. This is the reason—or at least a big part of the reason—why, in capitalist economies, the poor are becoming poorer while the rich are becoming richer and the middle class is shrinking. Marxist economies, on the other hand, have a mechanism for assuring access to subsistence goods, but it is at the cost of denying a most basic and precious transcendence need: freedom of worship. One of the consequences is that Communist cultures end up imitating one of the worst features of capitalist societies—namely, an insatiable greed, which is signified as a virtue and a symbol of success so long as it is expressed by the state.

We will not get far in trying to find a Christian response to environmental questions if we divorce these from very concrete economic questions. To permit the separation would be to imitate the error of modern economics, so much of which tries to deal with goods and their production, distribution, and consumption, and which treats the individual as only a factor of the economic processes while ignoring the very features of the individual that make an economy worthwhile in the first place. Environmentalism will remain sterile or degenerate into romanticism if it shies away from a careful integration with the human.

So far I have argued that the church should teach interdependence and a development theory based on a view of reality that honors the primacy of the person in nature and in economic systems. Closely related to this is the next area that cries out to the church for help: work. Our society needs a theology of work. I suspect that if any of us consulted a random sampling of our neighbors about their reasons for working, most of them would say that they work to earn a living. To espouse such a truncated vision of the purpose of working is to condemn oneself to a way of living that is cut off from most of the glory of being alive; it is also to threaten the environment. If we work only to earn a living, then what is to stop us from taking and using anything we can get our hands on to make that living? Where can we find norms for putting a ceiling on the material standard of living?

A Christian view of work equips us with a set of habits and attitudes conducive to profound reverence for all that we handle. We can see this clearly by examining four purposes of work.

First, by our work we complete God's creation. In the eucharistic liturgy we pray over bread and wine as "fruit of the earth and work of human hands." If we are to live, we must rework nature as we meet it, and this was never more true than today, when we have so many people sharing the resources of the planet. It would be devastating if we tried to get our drinking water directly from springs, or relied only on animal power for energy. It may be worthwhile to experiment with living in close and immediate dependence on nature on a temporary basis, as I discovered on two separate occasions when I lived in a hermitage for a month. But for millions of people to live that way on a permanent basis would be impossible.

The church can do much to help us live in the ambiance of the great truth that we are working with God, and in a very real way that God is working with us and in us. This is not a realm of mystery someplace in the stratosphere, but a realm that we live in every day of our lives. If I have a keen and lasting sense of the truth of my situation as someone working with God, collaborating in completing the creation, I will intuitively approach my work with a sense of its importance and also of my own. I will find that I instinctively shy away from the shoddy, the dishonest, the injurious, the cavalier, and the careless.

Think, for example, of what we know of Jesus and his ways of dealing with the fruits of the earth and the work of human hands, of his directing the disciples to gather the fragments after the feeding of the multitude, of his knowledge and appreciation of the agricultural methods of his day. Remember how consistently he drew attention to the truth that we do not need everything that we can get our hands on; moreover, we imperil our lives by greed. This point is brought home to us by the story of the rich young man and by the parable about the man who died the night he finished building his new enlarged storage barns.

We are also taught the unmistakably clear lesson that we must relate to the environment and do our work always guided by the subsistence needs of all others in light of being taught to know God as our Father. Think of the story of the rich man and Lazarus, of the Good Samaritan, or of the last judgment in Matthew 25, in which Jesus makes it clear that God must be recognized as integral to our economic process, and that our eternal destiny depends on acting on this recognition. He will say, "I was hungry and you gave me food. . . . Come," or "I was hungry and you never gave me food. . . . Depart."

The first purpose of work is to complete God's creation, and the second purpose is to complete our very selves. Like the rest of creation, we come into being unfinished, and like the rest of creation, of which we are a part, the completion is not automatic, easy, or free from hazards. As Paul told the community of Antioch, "We all have to experience many hardships before we enter the kingdom of God" (Acts 14:22). Elsewhere Paul reminded the Ephesians that "we are God's work of art" (Eph. 2:10).

We have all experienced the truth that we make ourselves by our work and that there is no other way to do it. We discover and develop our powers by exercising them, whether it be the power to type, to paint, to make a long-range plan, to teach a class, or to write an article. Without work we would quickly become retarded human beings, completely dependent on others to tend our needs until we died—a very sorry prospect. An important part of the church's ministry is to hold before us the vision of our vocation, of the kind of people we are called to be and to become, so that we can have a picture of the kind of world we should be about. We are called to be disciples of Jesus, and therefore to learn by association with him the kind and manner of our own work. Clearly, we are to work with unfailing care and concern especially for the poor and the oppressed. We are not to work for ourselves, and we are to work as servants, out of love. The mysterious and perhaps threatening episode of the footwashing of the apostles as recorded in the Gospel according to John reminds us of the attitude that we should have in working for others.

The third purpose of our work is to bring us into communion with our brothers and sisters; it is a cure for loneliness, for isolation. Today more than ever before, so much depends on team enterprises. Teamwork is another facet of our interdependence. As goods are intended not to be possessed but to be shared, so work itself is meant to bring us into those relationships on which our very personhood depends. Even the solitary individual working in a research laboratory or writing in a study is called by the work itself into communion with others for whom the research or writing is intended.

The fourth purpose of our work is to provide the goods and services that the human family needs. In today's intricate network of economic relationships, our work may directly touch the lives of people who live on the other side of the planet and whom we will never see. We need to recognize that we often enjoy the goods that come our way at the expense of the injustices and oppressions inflicted on so many of the world's poor. We cannot rectify or even avoid each injustice, but this fourth purpose of work makes us face up to our responsibility to be doing something concrete and constructive to further economic and social justice on both local and global levels. This consideration may also help us face the uncomfortable truth that some of our economic practices are directly related to harmful environmental practices. Actually, this is true of so much of our economy. We need the church to help us live faithfully in the truth that we are called to live lives of caring, not to benefit from the rape of other people's lands and the exploitation of cheap labor.

How should the church teach? Perhaps an incident from the life of Gandhi will help answer the question:

> During the thirties a woman came to Sevegram asking Gandhi to get her little boy to stop eating sugar; it was doing him harm. Gandhi gave a cryptic reply: "Please come back next week."
> The woman left puzzled but returned a week later, dutifully following the Mahatma's instructions. "Please don't eat sugar," Gandhi told the young fellow when he saw him. "It is not good for you." Then he joked with the boy for a while, gave him a hug and sent him on his way. But the mother, unable to contain her curiosity, lingered behind to ask, "Bapu, why didn't you say this last week when we came? Why did you make us come back again?"
> Gandhi smiled. "Last week," he said to her, "I too was eating sugar."[6]

The church has a teaching role in healing the earth, but it must be first and foremost by way of example, by way of witness. The earth, after all, is the victim of wounds that we ourselves have helped to inflict. Some of us are seriously compromised in our efforts to work for justice and peace—including environmental issues—by our own violations of the very practices we advocate. The fact that we do not always recognize our inconsistencies does not remove them or eliminate the harm they do to others and to our potential effectiveness.

Our reform cannot be a single act of repentance, though it must begin there. Rather, we must dedicate ourselves to a continuing conversion, and that in turn will require that we partici-

---

6. Eknath Easwaran, *Gandhi the Man* (Petaluma, Calif.: Nilgiri Press, 1978), pp. 170-71.

pate with others who are also concerned about the healing of the earth.

One way of specifying our resolve to speak from a position of consistency is to enter into a covenant relationship with others who are on a similar journey. Today there is a growing covenant relationship among thousands of Christians who are committed to the abolition of nuclear weapons. The theology of this New Abolitionist Covenant can also undergird our effort to bring our Christian vision and our effort to live faithfully to bear on the environmental issues. The six areas of practice specified in the text of this covenant—prayer, education, spiritual examination, peace evangelism, public witness, and nuclear disarmament—likewise apply. This is not surprising, since the existence of nuclear weapons is the single most vivid expression of sinfulness regarding the environment.

Linking environmental issues with issues of disarmament is as necessary as linking disarmament and abortion. In all these issues we work from a foundation of belief in the sanctity of life, crowned by human life made in the very image of God, and therefore crowned with glory and honor. When working for particular legislative targets, we need to sharpen our focus and organize to lobby for very specific measures. On the educational level, however, we do well to bring issues together and to clarify their linkage at the deepest level of value and belief.

Too often in our efforts to shape public policy we have not paid adequate attention to understanding the foundation of a position taken, and have instead invested disproportionate amounts of energy in trying to win support for or against specific policies or pieces of legislation. The result is that we have a plethora of single-issue causes, organizations, and campaigns. Many people of good will join none of them because they have no criteria for choice. They fear that once they begin, they won't know when or where to stop. How many times have we heard a person with genuine concern for issues of social justice and peace say, "I can't join all the groups that ask me to join and support them. I can't even keep up with their mail, and I don't know which one or two I can best support, or where my contribution could be most effective." In the next ten years, all those involved professionally in any issue of peace and justice should commit themselves to investing a higher proportion of their time and energy to finding ways of shaping a vision of the kingdom of peace and justice and ways of helping others understand their calling to participate in the building of a human environment open to the inbreaking of this kingdom. Then we might see, by the end of the decade, more policymakers who can be counted on to exert leadership in the entire arena of peace and social justice.

* * *

I have presented three models or symbols for the church—the church as a community of disciples, as mother, and as teacher—and three modes of response to environmental issues suggested by these models: contemplation, compassionate care, and education on interdependence and the meaning of human work. I have addressed the mystery of suffering implicit in the idea that the church is called to heal, and to heal in the way of Jesus: by bearing the wounds of our situation in love, a love grounded in faith and hope. Our belief and our hope is that our destiny is to participate in the new creation.

Creation, Church,
and
Christian Responsibility

LARRY L. RASMUSSEN

Early on, when time and earth were yet young, they all gathered
about dawn: the dragonflies and blackbirds, the Swedish ivies
and Boston ferns (though they weren't yet sure about Sweden
and Boston), the tyrannosaurus rexes and the duck-billed
platypuses, a lion and a lamb, a woman heavy with child and a
shy young man, and of course, the elder among them—Venus,
the morning star. They waited. They all waited to see if it would
happen again. With growing impatience they waited. And waited, ever so long. Finally it happened. They broke into applause,
grabbed one another by the arm (or wing, or frond, or whatever),
did a joyful jig, and sang a funny-sounding song. It had really
happened again! The sun had come up one more time. And in
almost the very same place. Morning had broken, just like the
first morning.

As was now their habit, they elected a Village Philosopher
for the day and retired to the daily session of the Primitive Theology Brunch Bunch Discussion Group. It had one and only one
question that it loved to contemplate: Why is there something

LARRY L. RASMUSSEN *is the Reinhold Niebuhr Professor of Social Ethics at
Union Theological Seminary in New York. He is also a member of the Standing
Committee of the Office of Church in Society, an organization of the American
Lutheran Church. He is the author of* Economic Anxiety and Christian Faith
(Augsburg, 1981), and co-author, with Bruce C. Birch, of Bible and Ethics in
the Christian Life *(Augsburg, 1976) and* The Predicament of the Pros-
perous *(Westminster Press, 1978).*

rather than nothing? And the glow of that astonishing occur-
rence—the rising of the sun—stayed with them the day long.

But soon some grew bored. They quit coming to the regular
midmorning discussion group with its one and only question.
They quit gathering at dawn. Some claimed an inalienable right
to sleep in. Soon they quit applauding and dancing and singing.
There were other things to do—toil, reap, cook, complain, invent
aspirin, suffer ulcers and coronaries. God continued doing only
wonders, but no one noticed. They would wake up alive but fail
to be astonished at that; see one another, alive and well, but
hardly let the mystery of it all register; eat and drink and kiss
good-bye on the way to the bus, all without a single ounce of awe.
Birthing, breathing, laughing, crying, singing, working, dying—
it all went on. God kept doing only wonders, mornings like the
first morning, but no one gathered to feel creation anew. They
even forgot the question they loved to contemplate: Why is there
something rather than nothing?

* * *

This preface is meant to express the gracious giftedness of
creation and lead into a discussion of human response and responsibility—specifically, the relationship of creation and the
community called the church. The overall framework is established by two running themes in the charter documents of Christian faith, the Hebrew Scriptures (the Old Testament) and the
apostolic writings (the New Testament): (1) the origin and destiny
of creation as God's, and (2) the formation and vocation of witnessing communities. These themes in turn mark out two arenas
of Christian responsibility: (1) the care of creation, at least that
patch of creation affected by human power, and (2) the community of faith. Sometimes the designation is "Israel among the nations," sometimes "the church in the world." In both cases the
called-out character of the assembly (ek-klesia) entails a particular
vocation. And that vocation involves a moral stance, a way of life,
an ethic.

THE THEOLOGICAL FRAMEWORK

One way to explore the theological framework of this ethic is to
track some crucial words—"creation," "neighbor," "justice,"
"peace," "church." They bear meanings to think *with*; they are
not simply concepts to think *about*. Indeed, any time we think
about things—such as human responsibility—it is our "think

with's" that guide the process and shape the outcome. These key meanings make up the controlling framework within which we think about things. They provide an interpretive scheme for weighing and understanding our experience.

Creation

"Creation" is a theological word—that is, its meaning is in view of *God's* reality. It is the theological word for the totality of all things (in Greek, *ta panta*). Had Hebrews been asked about creation, they would have pointed to land, livestock, health, family, tools, commerce, governing institutions, village and city and countryside, patterns of relationship and social traffic, rocks, trees, and wild animals, sun, moon, and stars, even their cursed enemies—all things except God, the Creator. More precisely, all things together *in relation to* God.

Strictly speaking, "creation" is our term, and not in the Old Testament sense. The verb form, "creating," is common in the Scriptures. But a noun form used to refer to some vast entity is absent, which only underscores the sense of the Creator's ongoing creating and sustaining—indeed, underscores the unfinished character of the world. "Ongoing created order" might better convey the reality here, provided the phrase carries a sense of energy, dynamism, and change, as well as suggests persisting patterns that conserve and preserve.

In any event, there is a vision that the ongoing created order, for all its fecund diversity of form and kind, is of a piece. Walter Brueggemann says it succinctly: "The central vision of world history in the Bible is that all creation is one, every creature in community with every other, living in harmony and security toward the joy and well-being of every other creature."[1] This vision is nicely reflected in one of the many biblical ways of imaging the world—as an *oikos* (house). Creation is pictured as a vast public household. The English words "economics," "ecumenics," and "ecology" all share this root and reference. "Economics" means providing for the household's material and service needs and managing the household well. But the word also has a theological meaning. One of the classic theological expressions for bringing creation to full health is the unfolding drama of "the divine economy" *(oikonomia tou Theou)*. One of the

---

1. Brueggemann, *Living Toward a Vision: Biblical Essay on Shalom* (New York: United Church Press, 1976), p. 15.

marks of that economy is shared abundance. "Ecumenics" means treating the inhabitants of the household as a single family, human and nonhuman together, and fostering the unity of that family. "Ecology" is knowledge of that systemic interdependence upon which the life of the household depends. And if English had adopted the Greek word for steward (*oikonomos*), we would immediately recognize the steward as the trustee, the caretaker of creation imaged as an *oikos*.

For the 1972 conference on the environment sponsored by the United Nations, scientist René Dubos and economist Barbara Ward wrote the following, in striking confirmation of this ancient, unitary understanding of the created order:

> There is something clarifying and irresistible in plain scientific fact. The astonishing thing about our deepened understanding of reality over the last four or five decades is the degree to which it confirms and reinforces so many of the older moral insights of humanity. The philosophers told us we were one, part of a greater unity that transcends our local drives and needs. They told us that all living things are held together in a most intricate web of interdependence. They told us that aggression and violence, blindly breaking down the delicate relationships of existence, could lead to destruction and death. These were, if you like, intuitions drawn in the main from the study of human societies and behaviour. What we now learn is that they are factual descriptions of the way in which our universe actually works.[2]

Neighbor

"Who is my neighbor?" and "Am I my neighbor's keeper?" are basic questions when the subject is moral responsibility and Christian vocation. The meaning of "neighbor" follows from the understanding of creation. Neighbor is a "universal" term: all are neighbors. Jesus voices the radical reach of this when he construes the enemy as neighbor and instructs his followers to treat all neighbors with a regard equal to that which they accord themselves and their closest compatriots. Nor are contemporaries, whether near or far, friend or foe, our only neighbors. Unborn generations are neighbors as well, as are past generations. Moral responsibility stretches through time and arches across space.

Rarely has anyone articulated the understanding of "neighbor" as succinctly or as well as H. Richard Niebuhr has.

---

2. Dubos and Ward, *Only One World* (London: Penguin Books, 1972), p. 85.

He wrote the following (taken from *The Purpose of the Church and Its Ministry*) in the 1950s, before the rise of the environmental movement and during an intensification of the Cold War between the United States and the U.S.S.R. That he did so shows that the roots of this understanding are in Jewish and Christian tradition, roots that penetrate deeper than the soil of American culture.

> Who, finally, is my neighbor, the companion whom I have been commanded to love as myself? [The neighbor] is the near one and the far one; the one removed from me by distances in time and space, in convictions and loyalties. . . . The neighbor is in past and present and future, yet [the neighbor] is not simply [humankind] in its totality but rather in its articulation, the community of individuals in community. [The neighbor] is Augustine in the Roman Catholic Church and Socrates in Athens, and the Russian people, and the unborn generations who will bear the consequences of our failures, future persons for whom we are administering the entrusted wealth of nature and other greater common gifts. [The neighbor] is [humanity] and [the neighbor] is angel and [the neighbor] is animal and inorganic being, all that participates in being.[3]

The neighbor is "all that participates in being." That's everything!

But how is the neighbor to be treated? Jesus' teaching in the Sermon on the Mount (Matthew 5-7, with parallels in Luke) sets the basic stance and terms. The discussion is neighbor love; the subject is the enemy. To this discussion we will add the subject of this book: the care of the good earth.

What is initially striking is Jesus' contrast of neighbor love with the common experience of love. We love those close to us who return our affection and with whom we identify—family, friends, tribe, nation. When Jesus includes love of the enemy as the sure test of love's authenticity, then the nature of this love becomes clear. Simply put, it means that there are no grounds of any kind for setting aside *any* neighbor as an exception to the command to love. If the enemy is *included*, no one is *excluded*, since the enemy is the one most likely to be an exception.

What is striking as well is the simplicity of neighbor love. We usually associate love with an emotional bond to another or

---

3. Niebuhr et al., *The Purpose of the Church and Its Ministry: Reflections on the Aims of Theological Education* (New York: Harper & Row, 1956), p. 38. I have substituted some words to avoid sexist terms.

others, some attachment of empathy and unity. Common love normally roots in something important held in common—family, culture, citizenship, shared hopes and values. But enemy love would hardly be an emotional bond of affection. It hardly springs from unity, empathy, or commonality. For Jesus, neighbor love—with enemy love as the litmus test of its reality—is simply seeking the welfare and serving the needs of others as we would seek and serve our own. Strong emotions may be part of this love, of course, but it has no required emotional prerequisites. Nor is moral heroism required. Granted, emotions and moral reach might be shaped and changed by loving on these terms. But the steady center is simply imitating the kind of love God manifests. (As Paul wrote to the Romans, "While we were yet enemies, God reconciled us"; 5:10.) Indeed, loving the enemy does not deny that the relationship is one of enmity. It names it for what it is and tries to express love within it by putting the enemy's needs and status on a par with one's own ("*While* we were yet enemies . . .").

This can be expressed in another way. God's way in Jesus is to create community by joining the struggle against its greatest flaws: the exclusion of some from the ranks of the rest, and the fostering of "tribalism" on that basis. For this reason, the Beatitudes are good news, Gospel: the formerly excluded—the poor, the meek, the persecuted, the peacemakers—are now included and accorded the radical equality of neighbor love. Community is whole. With that, a patch of creation is healed. Community that is partial is a literal contradiction. It is creation still broken.

If we transfer this perspective to care of the environment, recalling that the neighbor is "all that participates in being," the moral reasoning would go like this. To love nonhuman life—even inorganic being—as neighbor does not require commonality, unity, or even bonds of affection, though we may and ought to learn from traditions that nurture these between us and our co-siblings of creation. Nor does loving the nonhuman created order require proximity in time and space. We can love the good earth of and for future generations just as we can care for portions of the planet we never see. The simplicity of neighbor love applies: we should put the welfare and needs of nonhuman others in the same frame of reference as our own welfare and needs. This will not render decision-making easier, because needs are frequently competitive and interests often clash. Sacrifice and compromise are real and necessary. But it does clarify and simplify the shape of moral responsibility when, as a matter of ecological fact, all things *are* interrelated.[4]

Justice

While the vision of redeemed creation is that of harmonious, abundant, and secure life together, our actual experience of the world is creation broken, laced with deep discord, stirred by profound need and want. Fissures of suffering, pain, and violation rend nature, psyche, and society every bit as often as joy, ecstasy, and satisfaction surface.

Our ancestors in the faith knew the same experience and had a way of understanding it. The Hebrews shared with other peoples of the ancient Near East a cosmology that went something like this. The creation of the universe by the gods or God was a mighty movement from chaos—matter as "formless and void"—to harmonious order. Yet chaos continually intrudes. The struggle between chaos and creation is joined and never ceases in the experience of the world as we know it. The forms of chaos are many: famine and hunger, plagues and disease, mental illness, marital and generational estrangement, deceitfulness and corruption, denial of goods to those in genuine need, and so forth. "Sin" is one name for this deep, pervasive disorder. It is the triumph, however temporary, of an always threatening chaos. It is the presence of evil in nature, psyche, and society, and it is the enemy of the ongoing created order.

Hebrew thinking about justice reflects this portrayal of reality. Justice does not first appear as a concept of the great prophets of the sixth and eighth centuries B.C.; it stems from an older understanding of cosmic reality as harmonious world order. When the Hebrew confession says again and again that Yahweh is "just," it means that God fashions order from chaos, holds back the chaos, and balances things anew when chaos intrudes. Justice is the achievement of harmony, often through severe measures. (In the prophetic oracles, nations and empires fall when their injustice provokes God's "imbalancing" wrath. In Mary's song, echoing Hannah's, the poor are exalted, and the rich are sent away empty.)

Since Hebrew minds were not given to separate history

---

4. For this discussion of neighbor love, I am indebted to John Howard Yoder, "Jesus' Life-Style Sermon and Prayer," in *Social Themes of the Christian Year: A Commentary on the Lectionary*, ed. Dieter T. Hessel (Philadelphia: Geneva Press, 1983), pp. 87-96.

from nature (there is not even a Hebrew word to name nonhuman nature), justice does not participate in such a separation. Differently said, justice does not refer only to human relationships and human events. Its many-sidedness may refer one time to human events (tossing Pharaoh's horses and riders into the sea) and another time to phenomena we assign to nature (the Flood). Moreover, the many dimensions forbid using a single word to bear the full notion of justice. Sometimes *sedeqah* (righteousness) is used, sometimes *hesed* (loving-kindness); elsewhere it's *emet* (faithfulness), *tom* (completeness, integrity), *miswah* (order), *torah* (instruction), *shalom* (peace, wholeness), or *mishpat* (equity, "justice"). Nonetheless, there is a comprehensive meaning here, which Paul Wee formulates as follows: "Justice . . . is the right and harmonious ordering of life in all its dimensions under the sovereignty of God, wherein the creative harmony, which continues to exist in essence under the conditions of sinful existence, is reflected."[5]

Such an understanding of justice needs a further word. It is a more comprehensive understanding of justice than that which reigns in Anglo-American moral traditions. Those traditions have defined justice as liberty or equality or some combination of these. Justice as liberty means guaranteeing the widest range of individual choice commensurate with such choice for others. Justice as equality means guaranteeing a comparative allotment of goods, services, and opportunities at a humane level for the largest number possible. Much debate, legislation, and policy formulation turns on which concept will prevail and the ways in which one concept might complement or correct the other. Incidentally, it should not escape our notice that both concepts share a common anthropocentrism. They assume the sphere of justice is populated only by humans and pertains only to *human* welfare, directly or indirectly.

Creation pictured as an *oikos* does not eliminate concern for liberty and equality, much less for human welfare in general. But the basic "unit" of reality is the whole creation in God. It is not the individual nor even humanity as a species. *Justice,* biblically, *is the rendering,* amidst limited resources and the conditions of brokenness, *of whatever is required for the fullest possible flourishing of creation.* That which makes for wholeness in nature, psyche, and society is "just."

5. Wee, in Sibusiso Bengu, *Mirror or Model? The Church in an Unjust World* (New York: Lutheran World Ministries, 1984), pp. 8-9.

Peace

The content of justice introduces another "think with"— *shalom*. Though most often rendered "peace," *shalom* is really shorthand for all God's hopes and dreams for creation. It is shared abundance and full health in every sphere. It is well-being extended to all creatures so that life is lived without debilitating fear. It is tranquility and serenity. And it is more. It is bread; it is dance.

The antonym of *shalom* is chaos and anomie. Perhaps better said, it is the myriad forms of violence that exist. Positively, *shalom*-making runs the gamut of human activities: planting and harvesting, commerce, child-rearing and parent-caring, making friends, making treaties, making love, making music, caring for victims, building productive human institutions, offering security and protection, providing bodily care, nurturing the spirit, celebrating the rites of passage and the stages of life, and so forth. All that intersects the cure and care of creation belongs to peace-making and peacekeeping.

Shalom, then, is considerably more than the avoidance of war and the limiting of violence. But it must quickly be added that the ancient understanding of peace—the well-being of creation—and the ancient understanding of threats to it—the intrusion of chaos—have a stark, direct relevance in our ultramilitarized world. Weapons of mass destruction—especially nuclear, chemical, and biological weapons—pose the unprecedented possibility of a cataclysmic victory of chaos over that piece of creation which is our only home. No previous war, however horrible its local manifestation, carried the awesome capacity to draw the curtain on the very *possibility* of having neighbors in the future. No previous war had the capacity to render the planet itself virtually dead and its atmosphere hostile to the fertile evolution of teeming life. None could transform this patch of rich creation into little more than a cinder, its magnificent past to be carried only in the memory of God. The literal meaning of "holocaust" is too real a possibility: the consumption, by fire, of all that is. Nature is indeed astonishingly resilient, and God is utterly irrepressible. But there are limits to the power of both, and we, like Jesus, live with the sovereignty of God contested. God's ways can be frustrated by our ways, at least for planet earth.

Thus, while the full meaning of *shalom* is far-reaching and total well-being, its minimum definition is the avoidance of nuclear fire and the biochemical devastation of the environment. "Greenpeace" becomes a matter of Christian political responsibility.

Church

"Church" may not be the best term. Earlier I used "community of faith" and "witnessing communities." Most of the biblical drama is, after all, the story of Israel's pilgrimage and the story of a Jew, Jesus of Nazareth. Yet this book is directed to Christian communities in particular. The vocation of the church, both early and present, commands our attention.

Nonetheless, whether Israel or the church, the vocation is the same: to witness to God's hope for *all* by living as *communities of visibly redeemed creation.* The believing community is to display in its own life the justice-doing and peacemaking of God. It is to be an anticipatory community of creation-made-new, a taste or aperitif of the reign of God. Differently said, it is to be a restored society. This is the point that Karl Barth makes in his *Church Dogmatics:*

> The decisive contribution which the Christian community can make to the upbuilding and work and maintenance of the civil [order] consists in the witness which it has to give to it and to all human societies in the form of the order of its own upbuilding and constitution. It cannot give in the world a direct portrayal of Jesus Christ, who is also the world's Lord and Savior, or of the peace and freedom and joy of the kingdom of God. For it is itself only a human society moving like all others to [God's] manifestation. But in the form in which it exists among them it can and must be to the world . . . around it a reminder of the law of that kingdom of God already set up on earth in Jesus Christ, and a promise of its future manifestation. *De facto,* whether they realize it or not, it can and should show them that there is already on earth an order which is based on the great alteration of the human situation and directed towards its manifestation.[6]

This means the community's own formation is a vital zone of responsibility. In fact, Christian social ethics has a double focus: the first arena of action is the concrete organization of the imitation of God and of Christ in the world *as shalom community;* the second is the relationship of that piece of world called "church" to its wider environment and the far-reaching exercise of human responsibility there. Barth makes this comment: "If the community were to imagine that the reach of the sanctification of humanity accomplished in Jesus Christ were restricted to itself and the ingathering of believers, that it did not have correspond-

---

6. Barth, quoted by Stanley Hauerwas in *The Peaceable Kingdom: A Primer in Christian Ethics* (Notre Dame: University of Notre Dame Press, 1983), pp. 166-67.

ing effects *extra muros ecclesiae,* it would be in flat contradiction to
its own confession of its Lord."[7]

The biblical community's experience is again instructive for
our thinking. The Exodus—the initial, formative event of people-
hood in the Hebrew Scriptures—led inevitably to a question:
How do we embody now, in our life together, the freedom won
for us by this liberating, people-making God? "Sinai" inaugu-
rated the answer. The social task in the wilderness was to fashion, amid forbidding and alien circumstances, a faithful
community that took its cues from the experience of God's
mighty presence. Freedom *from* had to issue in freedom *for* and *to;*
freedom had to find social form. This wilderness task, continuing
in the new land, addressed a set of questions that recur in com-
munity-building almost anywhere. What will be the community's economics? Its polity and politics? Its ritual and worship? Its
social intercourse and the nature of its ties to its neighbors? Who
will perform what tasks of livelihood and governance in family
and clan? How will work be assigned and the benefits and bur-
dens distributed? What laws will prevail, and how will law-
breakers be treated?

For the Hebrews, forging answers meant paying attention
to a mix of factors: local conditions, memory, human imagination, and a conviction that the community should reflect in its
own character and conduct the character and conduct of the
righteous and compassionate God. The collective moral reasoning of these tribes of Yahweh went something like this. If the
majestic and elusive presence we call Yahweh redeemed the poor
and knew our suffering as the marginalized—as slaves, widows,
and orphans—we too should show compassion and redeem the
victim and the excluded. If the mighty Yahweh visited us as
strangers in the land of Egypt and showed us saving hospitality,
we in turn must not oppress the stranger but offer hospitality.
Indeed, we should bear a compassion and righteousness like
unto God's very own, and love our neighbor, including the
stranger, as ourselves. We should welcome even our enemy into
covenant intimacy.

The legislation that fills page upon page of Exodus, Leviticus, and Deuteronomy was in part an effort to reflect the experience and character of God in the social formation of the new
community. That the whole endeavor also smacked of human
frailty, error, and even narrow and corrupting perspectives and

---

7. Barth, cited in *The Peaceable Kingdom,* p. 167.

practices is hardly a surprise, given the tenacious hold of sin in every generation of which we have a record.

Similar dynamics were present in the early church. The community's experience of the resurrected Jesus and the giving of the Spirit led to the establishment of very practical tasks in answer to a question: How do we now embody the intense reality of the living Christ among us, in the reality of our ongoing, day-to-day life together? What will we do with our goods, our houses, our land? How will we organize fellowship with one another, locally and across distances—that is, how will we "break bread together" as members of the same Body who live in different nations? What should be the form of governance among us? How will worship be conducted and the rituals of our former lives be appropriated or discarded? What will we say to Caesar and his army? To the tax collectors? What about the relationship of parents to children, of husbands to wives, of masters to slaves? What are the terms of membership in the community, and how should we treat those who transgress community ways? How should we treat those who take offense at us and persecute us?

Like the Sinai responses, these efforts bore the marks of limited human vision and limited cooperation. The life of the early church was marred by finitude and parochialism. Nonetheless, the salient point is that the efforts cannot be understood apart from the empowering experience of Jesus, undeniable in the community's experience, vindicated in the resurrection, and vivified in the Spirit. The imitation of Christ, the "putting on" and "following" of Christ, became the way this new called-forth assembly *(ekklesia)* carried on the imitation of God. Jesus was Pattern, Teacher, Example, the fullest possible incarnation of God's nature in human form.

In both cases—Israel and the early church—the social creation of the community's own life was tied inextricably to its religious experience. The community itself was the subject of direct, formative moral responsibility. Theology, as reflection on faith for guidance in the Christian life, was a most practical discipline. When members of the faith community contemplated their moral responsibility, they did not ask "What is the universal good, and what action on our part would be in accord with it?" They asked, in effect, "What action on our part is in keeping with who we are as the people of God?"[8] The church in its origins

8. See the discussion in Bruce C. Birch and Larry L. Rasmussen, *Bible and Ethics in the Christian Life* (Minneapolis: Augsburg Publishing House, 1976), pp. 125ff.

did not so much *have* a social ethic as it *was* a social ethic *in formation.*

THE NEW CREATION AND THE CHURCH

We have gathered some strands or key concepts: the ongoing created order, the neighbor, justice, peace, the church—strands that carry moral content for our own setting. And we have designated two broad zones of Christian responsibility: the believing community's own life, and the life of the wider world of which it is an inextricable part. Yet to fully understand these responsibilities requires further comment.

Christian faith is an eschatological faith. As Stanley Hauerwas points out, it views creation "in terms of a story, with a beginning, a continuing drama, and an end." And the end is decisive for the entire tale. The future has the power to shape the present, and the past and the present derive meaning from their future.[9] More than that, however, the future from which Christian faith views the world is frequently in conflict with the present patterns of social life. Christian faith was born amid cries of clashing epochs and the intrusion of a new reality. Jesus' preaching is of the kingdom to come. New Age/Old Age, New Humanity, New Creation, disengagement from "the pattern of this present age," way of life/way of death, life in the flesh/life in the spirit—all this talk of struggle and birth is typical, rather than abnormal, apostolic talk. Scripture makes it clear that the church in its origins understood itself as a community of the New Age and as a sojourning people. Sometimes the imagery is changed—John prefers images of light and darkness—but the same intrusion of a qualitatively different reality is claimed and proclaimed.

This qualitatively different reality is nonetheless the tale for all creation. The claim is that what one sees in the way of Jesus of Nazareth is what God struggles to gain for all creation. Jesus' life, as Hauerwas notes, "is the life of the end—this is the way the world is meant to be."[10] Furthermore, when Israel or the church or anyone else is faithful to the way of God in Jesus, they become part of the shared struggle for creation's redemption. When our faithfulness—or anyone else's—is like unto the faithfulness of Jesus, there God's kingdom is made visible, and there the social vocation of the church is fulfilled.

---

9. Hauerwas, *The Peaceable Kingdom*, p. 82.
10. Hauerwas, *The Peaceable Kingdom*, p. 85.

Until the tale is wholly played out, however, the conflict of competing patterns continues. And it is this tension, expressive of eschatological faith, that sets the basic orientation of the church's relationship to the world. The church is not the kingdom. Indeed, when the kingdom is fully come, there will be no church! But the church is to reflect as best it can God's own way and be a provisional, partial expression of the kingdom. Christian ethics, then, is *living in the Old Age on the terms of the New*. That most of church history is testimony to the fatal compromise of living in the New Age on the terms of the Old is itself the harshest indictment of the church. Such compromise is, in fact, the abandonment of eschatological faith itself.

But what of the relationship of that piece of world called "church" to the wider world? Specifically, what must Christians do to give faithful social witness in the culture in which they find themselves if their faith is inherently eschatological? In *The Use of the Bible in Christian Ethics*, Thomas Ogletree cites two requisites:

> From the standpoint of concrete experience, two things would seem to be crucial: some degree of alienation from the institutional arrangements of the larger society, and deep involvement with a community which is engaged in developing qualitatively distinct alternatives to those arrangements. The alienation and the involvement provide points of contact for comprehending what the biblical texts are saying [as eschatological texts].[11]

Ogletree goes on to say that neither institutional alienation nor membership in alternative-creating communities "has been especially prominent in recent Christian ethics in America."[12] More commonly, American Christians have identified with the larger society, its problems and possibilities. (That Protestants have failed to organize their denominations along other than *national* lines as the strongest jurisdictional boundaries is one very telling piece of evidence.)

To sing the biblical melodies for the moral life means a different identification and a certain positioning, Ogletree says: "An eschatological orientation requires eschatological communities." Minimally, such communities "sustain hope in what is not yet"; optimally, they are anticipatory communities that "embody in their own life and activity features of the new age which are

---

11. Ogletree, *The Use of the Bible in Christian Ethics* (Philadelphia: Fortress Press, 1983), p. 182.
12. Ogletree, *The Use of the Bible in Christian Ethics*, p. 182.

present possibilities."[13] At this juncture, Ogletree's discussion is reminiscent of a passage from John Yoder's *Politics of Jesus:*

> There are thus about the community of disciples those sociological traits most characteristic of those who set about to change society: a visible structured fellowship, a sober decision guaranteeing that the costs of commitment to the fellowship have been consciously accepted, and a clearly defined life style distinct from that of the crowd. . . . The distinctness is not a cultic or ritual separation, but rather a nonconformed quality of ("secular") involvement in the life of the world. It thereby constitutes an unavoidable challenge to the powers that be and the beginning of a new set of social alternatives.[14]

Flannery O'Connor's quip comes to mind: "You shall know the truth and the truth shall make you odd."

Ogletree distinguishes two strains of biblical eschatology. "Futurist" eschatologies generate hope for a world that is not yet and that is not likely to emerge under conditions of severe oppression. But the faith refuses to yield sovereignty to the present age, and the believing community lives with an ethic of patient waiting and faithful enduring amid alien circumstances. Faith is holding out and holding on; it is utter refusal to be commandeered by a violent world. (The long, dark night of Ugandan Christians under the terror of Idi Amin comes to mind.) "Dialectical" eschatologies also envision the faithful community over against the present order, but with a difference. They see the opportunity for a transforming action whereby the community *can* create—at least to some degree—a social reflection of the kingdom in its own ranks, and *can* be an agent of transformation in its own wider world. (One example is the impact of the Radical Reformation's congregational polity upon budding democracy.)

There have been faith communities in North America so removed from the dominant culture that an ethic of patient enduring and of hope amid oppression, together with a refusal to yield ultimacy to the powers that be, was the lived ethic. The spirituals and the blues—indeed, much of the black church's experience—are potent testimony. Yet the more common cultural ethos has granted eschatological communities space to fashion styles of life distinct from and alternative to the culture's reigning arrangements. It is not opportunity and space that American Christians have lacked; it is the eschatological communities

---

13. Ogletree, *The Use of the Bible in Christian Ethics,* p. 185.
14. Yoder, *The Politics of Jesus* (Grand Rapids: Eerdmans, 1972), pp. 46-47.

themselves! The churches have so identified with the larger society (with the values and structures of democratic capitalism, for example) that an observer could easily conclude that the churches' operative calling has been to make *America* work better.

That is not wholly illegitimate. Christian faith does seek to relate positively to culture as well as take culture's measure with the prophet's plumb line. The church is called to care for and cure creation, and that means building up the life of the communities in which Christians find themselves while keeping in mind that the fundamental unit of reality is the whole creation. Yet the tension of eschatological faith is never resolved in such a way that faith offers a blanket ratification of any culture or any human institution—the nation and the church included.

THE LINES OF AN ENVIRONMENTAL ETHIC

Moral guidance derives in part from biblical and other resources of Christian faith. Some basic understandings, part of the faith itself, are the "think with's" that orient us *to* respond and that mold the nature of the response itself. Having discussed some of these meanings and having noted the church-and-culture dynamic of an eschatological faith, we conclude with lines of an ethic appropriate to the church's vocation and to environmental needs. They are Christian moral themes that converge with themes urged upon us by serious environmentalists everywhere.

A global consciousness should be part and parcel of our perception and decisions. Creation as the basic unit of reality means we should reach for increasingly inclusive frames of reference. Decision-making should be as universal as possible without being unworkably cumbersome.

Identification with the welfare of future generations should be nurtured and policies fostered that take their welfare into account together with our own. These are our neighbors. (A proverb nicely lifts this up as a matter of moral character: "When a man plants an olive tree under which he knows he will never sit, then civilization has come to that land.")

Perspectives should be fostered that regard humanity as an integral part of nature and that promote stewardly harmony with nature rather than conquest. Furthermore, material resource use should reward conserving rather than spending, preserving rather than discarding. A guideline question would be this: If my (our) standard of living were adopted by the whole world, would nature still flourish?

Policies and institutional forms should be found that reflect a conception of justice that takes into account the needs and "rights" of nonhuman as well as human creation. Nature is our neighbor too. We should work toward an informal (if not formal) bill of rights for nature as a whole.

Moral formation should include a keen sense of limits and knowledge of the fact that all behavior has environmental consequences. Child-rearing (and adult-rearing!) should include, in both formal and informal education and training, the inculcation of certain moral sensitivities: awe, reverence, gratitude, and vulnerability, among others. Creation is one, it is precious, and it is finite.

Such an ethic needs visible expression in communities willing to engage in a long season of experimentation and prefigure future possibilities. The church's vocation includes being such an anticipatory community. It should be one of those communities that demonstrates in its own ranks the possibilities of an environmental ethic.

* * *

This essay began in the language of image and narrative rather than of discourse and argument. This is also how it ends:

For as the rain and the snow come down from heaven,
    and return not thither but water the earth,
making it bring forth and sprout,
    giving seed to the sower and bread to the eater,
so shall my word be that goes forth from my mouth;
    it shall not return to me empty,
but it shall accomplish that which I purpose,
    and prosper in the thing for which I sent it.

For you shall go out in joy,
    and be led forth in peace;
the mountains and the hills before you
    shall break into singing,
    and all the trees of the field shall clap their hands.
Instead of the thorn shall come up the cypress;
    instead of the brier shall come up the myrtle;
and it shall be to the Lord for a memorial,
    for an everlasting sign which shall not be cut off.

(Isa. 55:10-13)

I've seen the mountains break forth into singing, and the trees clap their hands. The myrtle grows in Virginia, and in early

October you can actually embrace those soft, comfortable mountains. The dogwood go to oxblood, the gum trees to mottled black and red. The sumac flame red-orange, and the gold of the maples is straight from the painter's tube. The smell of hickory, embers fading to ashes, the last of the tomatoes in the garden, Sunday softball near the pumpkin patch, a butterfly or two, and October's long yellow light gently edging across rocking-chair porches. The feast of life; the gift of God. Receive it, celebrate it, share it, steward it.

Thirst

JOHN LEAX

1

No drought threatened
my father's land.

But when the dowser walked a grid
across the plot, the forked branch
gripped lightly in his hands
held steady in the air.

No flowing water would make
our habitation easy;
our lives would be sustained
by guile or skill.

To live by skill
required discipline,
the imposition of limits
before the imposition
of the end.

Habituated to the faucet's flow,
our minds could not acknowledge
the terms of earth.

We chose to live by guile.

JOHN LEAX is a poet, gardener, teacher, husband, father, and woodsman from the rolling hills of western New York. He is head of the Writing Department and poet-in-residence at Houghton College. His poetry has been published in many periodicals and issued in four collections. His latest titles are In Season and Out *(1985) and* The Task of Adam *(1985), published by Zondervan.*

2

The knowledge of cats,
of diesel engines
and digging deep
straight walls,
lived in my father's hands.

The big bucket clanging,
blue smoke chuffing
from the stack, he cut
fifteen feet into the shale.

He built a chambered cistern
larger than our whims.
But when the water passed
the level of enough,
the weight of excess
cracked the floor.

Brokenness returned
our minds to skill.
We learned to do
with little.

3

When winter rains
turned to blizzards
and the pump sucked air,
we hauled the lid aside
and shoveled snow
into the hole.

It mounded to the roof,
and we dropped
into the glow of snowy light
and threw the brightness
deeper into dark.

Hour after hour
we sweated warm
to drink depths
below the reach of frost.

4

The year it snowed on Easter
Father died before
the first purple crocus
affirmed the cyclic
resurrection of the year.

The cistern crack
heaved like a fault,
and our water ran
into the shale.

5

I climbed into the dry dark.

The square of light
falling on the floor
revealed the flaw,
the wild scrawl
of unbridled ambition.

In half-light, I picked
the thin line open wide
and stuffed the fissure
with waterplug.

My father's shadow
darkening my labor,
I knew the wealth
of water he imagined
could not be held.

I worked to stay the flow
enough to live
from rain to rain.

6

Nights later an early storm
swept up the valley.

At dawn, I rose,
went out,
and hand over hand,
lowered the measuring pole
into the dark.

In sunlight I read
the limit of my thirst
and vowed
to make enough
enough.

"A Handful of Mud":
A Personal History of My Love
for the Soil

PAUL W. BRAND

I grew up in the mountains of South India. My parents were
missionaries to the tribal people of the hills. Our own life was
about as simple as it could be, and as happy. There were no
roads. We never saw a wheeled vehicle except on our annual visit
to the plains. There were no stores, and we had no electricity and
no plumbing. My sister and I ran barefoot, and we made up our
own games with the trees and sticks and stones around us. Our
playmates were the Indian boys and girls, and our life was much
the same as theirs. We absorbed a great deal of their outlook and
philosophy, even while our parents were teaching them to read
and write and to use some of the tools from the West.

The villagers grew everything they ate, and rice was an
important food for all of us. The problem was that rice needs
flooded fields in the early stages of growth, and there was no
level ground for wet cultivation. So rice was grown all along the
course of streams that ran down gentle slopes. These slopes had
been patiently terraced hundreds of years before, and now every
terrace was perfectly level and bordered at its lower margin by an
earthen dam covered by grass. Each narrow dam served as a

PAUL W. BRAND *served for eighteen years at the Christian Medical College in
Vellore, India, pioneeering many innovative procedures and programs. He is
now the head of rehabilitation at the U.S. Public Health Service leprosy hospital
in Carville, Louisiana. Among his long list of honors and distinctions are the
prestigious Albert Lasker Award and his appointment as Commander of the
Order of the British Empire. He and Philip Yancey have co-authored two well-
known books published by Zondervan:* Fearfully and Wonderfully Made
(1980) and In His Image *(1984).*

footpath across the line of terraces, with a level field of mud and water six inches below its upper edge and another level terrace two feet below. There were no steep or high drop-offs, so there was little danger of collapse. If the land sloped steeply in one area, then the terraces would be very narrow, perhaps only three or four feet wide. In other areas where the land sloped very little, the terraces would be very broad. Every one of the narrow earth dams followed exactly the line of the contours of the slope.

Every few feet along every grassy path were little channels cut across the top of the dam for water to trickle over to the field below. These channels were lined with grass and were blocked by a grassy sod that the farmer could easily adjust with his foot to regulate the flow of water. Since each terrace was usually owned by a different family, it was important to have some senior village elder who would decide whether one farmer was getting too much or too little of the precious water supply.

Those rice paddies were a rich soup of life. When there was plenty of water, there would be a lot of frogs and little fish. Herons and egrets would stalk through the paddy fields on their long legs and enjoy the feast of little wrigglers that they caught with unerring plunges of their long beaks. Kingfishers would swoop down with a flash of color and carry off a fish from under the beak of a heron. And not only the birds enjoyed the life of the rice paddies—we boys did too. It was there that I learned my first lesson on conservation.

One day I was playing in the mud of a rice field with a half-dozen other little boys. We were catching frogs, racing to see who would be the first to get three. It was a wonderful way to get dirty from head to foot in the shortest possible time. But suddenly we were all scrambling to get out of the paddy. One of the boys had spotted an old man walking across the path toward us. We all knew him and called him "Tata," meaning "Grandpa." He was the keeper of the dams. He walked slowly, stooped over a bit, as though he were always looking at the ground. Old age is very much respected in India, and we boys shuffled our feet and waited in silence for what we knew was going to be a rebuke.

He came over to us and asked us what we were doing. "Catching frogs," we answered.

He stared down at the churned-up mud and flattened young rice plants in the corner where we had been playing, and I was expecting him to talk about the rice seedlings that we had spoiled. Instead he stooped and scooped up a handful of mud. "What is this?" he asked.

The biggest boy among us took the responsibility of answering for us all. "It's mud, Tata."

"Whose mud is it?" the old man asked.

"It's your mud, Tata. This is your field."

Then the old man turned and looked at the nearest of the little channels across the dam. "What do you see there, in that channel?" he asked.

"That is water, running over into the lower field," the biggest boy answered.

For the first time Tata looked angry. "Come with me and I will show you water."

We followed him a few steps along the dam, and he pointed to the next channel, where clear water was running. "That is what water looks like," he said. Then he led us back to our nearest channel, and said, "Is that water?"

We hung our heads. "No, Tata, that is mud, muddy water," the oldest boy answered. He had heard all this before and did not want to prolong the question-and-answer session, so he hurried on, "And the mud from your field is being carried away to the field below, and it will never come back, because mud always runs downhill, never up again. We are sorry, Tata, and we will never do this again."

But Tata was not ready to stop his lesson as quickly as that, so he went on to tell us that just one handful of mud would grow enough rice for one meal for one person, and it would do it twice every year for years and years into the future. "That mud flowing over the dam has given my family food every year from long before I was born, and before my grandfather was born. It would have given my grandchildren food, and then given their grandchildren food forever. Now it will never feed us again. When you see mud in the channels of water, you know that life is flowing away from the mountains."

The old man walked slowly back across the path, pausing a moment to adjust with his foot the grass clod in our muddy channel so that no more water flowed through it. We were silent and uncomfortable as we went off to find some other place to play. I had gotten a dose of traditional Indian folk education that would remain with me as long as I lived. Soil was life, and every generation was responsible for preserving it for future generations.

Over the years I have gone back to my childhood home several times. There have been changes. A road now links the hill people with the plains folk, for example. But traditional ways still continue. The terraced paddy fields still hold back the mud. Rice still grows in the same mud, and there is still an overseer called Tata—although he is one of the boys I used to play with sixty-five years ago. I am sure he lays down the law when he catches the boys churning up the mud, and I hope the system lasts for years to come. I have seen what happens when the old order breaks down, as it did in the Nilgiri Hills. I remember going there for a summer holiday with my family in 1921, when I was a boy.

The Nilgiri Hills, or Blue Mountains, were a favorite resort of the missionaries from the plains during the hot season. We hill folk did not need any change of climate, but we went because of the fellowship. The Nilgiris were steep and thickly forested, with few areas level enough for cultivation, even with terraces. The forestry service was strict and allowed no clearing of the trees except where tea plants or fruit or coffee trees were to be planted. These bushes and trees were good at holding soil, and all was well. I can remember, as a child, the clear streams and rivers that ran down the valleys, and the joy of taking a picnic to the waterfalls and wading in the pools.

Thirty years later—in the 1950s—I was back in India, now a doctor and a missionary myself, with a wife and a growing family. Now I was living on the hot plains at Vellore Christian Medical College. Everything about India brought back memories, but what I longed for most were the mountains, to remind me of my childhood. My wife and I started a tradition of taking our children to the Nilgiris every summer holiday, and they reveled in the cool air and enjoyed the forests and mountain peaks. But something was different, or soon became so.

A new breed of landowners began to take possession of the mountain forests. During the great struggle for independence in India, a number of people had suffered imprisonment, and they now claimed rewards from a grateful country. Free India had much goodwill but little money, so it gave land to these political sufferers, and some of that land was the forests of the Nilgiri Hills. These new landowners had not been farmers before. They had never known any Tata to teach them the value of mud. They wanted to make money, and make it fast. They knew that the climate was ideal for growing potatoes, and that there was a market for them. So they cleared forests from sloping land and planted potatoes. Two, even three crops could be harvested every year, and they made good money. But the land suffered. Harvesting potatoes involves turning over the soil, and monsoon rains often came before the new crop could hold the soil. . . .

One summer holiday our bus struggled up the winding road, and the heat of the plains gave way to cool breezes. We looked for the streams and waterfalls that I had loved. But now the water looked like chocolate syrup; it oozed rather than flowed. What we were seeing was rivers of mud. I felt sick.

There was a dear old Swiss couple, Mr. and Mrs. Fritschi, who lived in Coonoor, on the Nilgiri Hills. They had been missionaries of the Basel Mission in Switzerland but were long retired and now owned a nursery of young plants and trees. They loved to help and advise farmers and gardeners about ways to improve their crops. It seemed to me that these devoted people would know if there was some way to advise the landowners about ways to save their soil. I went to ask Mr. Fritschi about the havoc that was being wreaked by potato farming and to find out if there was anything that we could do. Mr. Fritschi despaired about the new landowners. His eyes were moist as he told me, "I have tried, but it is no use. They have no love of the land, only of money. They are making a lot of money, and they do not worry about the loss of soil because they think it is away in the future, and they will have money to buy more. Besides, they can deduct the loss of land from their income tax as a business depreciation." In the United States today this would be called agribusiness rather than farming, and indeed, the attitudes of agribusiness are much the same.

Thirty more years have passed, and my children have grown up and scattered, and we have left India. But we love it still, and every year I go back to visit my old medical college in Vellore and take part in the leprosy work there. I don't really enjoy going back to the Nilgiri Hills anymore, although many parts of them are still beautiful. I look up to the slopes that used to be covered with forests and then were planted with potatoes year after year. There are large areas of bare rock now, of no use to anybody. The deforested areas that still have some soil look like stretches of gravel. The streams and springs that ran off from these areas ran clear sixty years ago, flowed mud thirty years ago, and today are dry. When the rains come, they rush over this land in torrents; the land floods, then goes dry. . . . Oh, Tata! Where have you gone? You have been replaced by businessmen and accountants who have degrees in commerce and who know how to manipulate tax laws, by farmers who know about pesticides and chemical fertilizers but who care nothing about leaving soil for their great-grandchildren.

Down on the plains of India, where the land is flat, the

problems are different. Here too I have seen great changes in my lifetime. The biggest problem is population, and it keeps on growing. Here we doctors have to accept some responsibility, because we have helped to keep people alive who would have died without proper medical care. However, because of this improved care, families are getting smaller. Fewer children are lost to epidemics, and people are beginning to realize they do not need to have eight children to make sure two or three of them survive. It takes time for these facts to sink in, but we are seeing a reduction in birth rates, even though they still lag behind the drop in death rates. At the Vellore Christian Medical College we have active programs to help stabilize the population.

But the bottom line is that the population is still growing, and increasing population brings pressure to produce more food per acre of land. Many good ideas have helped to bring this about. New methods of cultivation from Japan and new strains of rice from the United States have begun what is called "the green revolution," which has been a wonderful boon to India. This green revolution has gotten a lot of publicity, but there has been less publicity focusing on the problems that nearly made it a disaster, and which still pose a warning for the future.

The new strains of rice produced a very high yield, but they were much less resistant to pests than the old strain of rice was, so farmers needed to use pesticides. The new rice also needed heavy doses of artificial fertilizers. Both the pesticides and the fertilizers were petroleum products, but that was no problem at first because the entire program was supported by overseas agencies. Fertilizers and pesticides were abundant.

The program went so well that it swept over the whole country, and everybody began using the new rice. But then the overseas support ran out, and at about the same time the price of petroleum rose, and suddenly India realized it could not afford to supply what the farmers all needed. There was a rush to go back to using the old rice which the farmers knew how to handle, and which did not need to be nurtured with expensive petroleum products. Panic struck when it seemed there was no old rice left, and farmers could not find seed stocks. Apparently, in the elation over the new rice, all the old seed stocks had been eaten.

As it turned out, not quite all the old rice was gone. Seed stocks were found, and the panic passed. Gradually other problems have been solved, at least for a time. Now other strains of rice are being used that have more of the good qualities of the old rice.

This taught me a lesson: there is real danger in losing the genetic resources that are in wild plants and in old tried-and-true crops. Today, in the excitement over the patented seeds produced by genetic splicing and the new hybrid strains of crops that produce high yields, we are losing seeds of ancient species. One day there will be no more petroleum, and one day many more insects will have developed resistance to our pesticides. Then we will look around wildly for seeds of plants that had the wisdom of the ages locked in their inheritance, and that knew how to handle the viruses and diseases that will plague us again—but these seeds will be gone. Through the problems of the green revolution I have sensed the panic we will then feel. Some new voluntary organizations are trying to anticipate this danger by developing seed banks, and I support them, my vivid memories convincing me of the validity of such efforts.

The availability of more food means more cooking, and that means more fuel. In India the traditional fuel is wood, and getting wood means losing trees. As I travel across India today, I miss the trees. Little by little the forests have disappeared. This time it is due less to rapacious landowners than to the housewives who need a bundle of firewood for the day's cooking. We have tried to teach better ways to make and use fire. In fact, many of the people in our district now use smokeless stoves instead of open fires for cooking, and they extract all the heat from their fuel before it becomes ash. But even so, the trees cannot keep up, because it seems that it's not anybody's job to be constantly replacing the trees that are cut down. True, the government does take some responsibility in this area. It at least takes great care of the huge shade trees—the banyans and tamarinds—that line both sides of the highways. These give shade and make it possible for bullock carts, cars, and especially pedestrians to move in comfort during the heat of the day. Because of the temptation to use even these key trees for firewood, the government has marked every one of them with a number that is boldly engraved into its trunk. Inspectors can travel all the roads and make sure no tree is missing. But some of these trees are dying, and everybody knows why.

As dusk falls along the road from Vellore to Madras, the crows begin to flock to roost in the trees, and the mynah birds sing their loud lullaby. Most people wind their way home as the sun goes down and work is finished. There are no streetlights, and the bullock carts keep going their plodding way with only kerosene lanterns to light their way. At intervals along the way I see women move over to the road with baskets under their arms and crooked knives under the folds of their saris. They squat down beside the road and wait. . . .

Each one is waiting for dark and quiet. When that comes, each moves up to one of the great trees and brings out the knife that Indians use for many purposes, rather like the machete of Mexico. She does not want much—just a basket full of bark and twigs that she can swiftly cut from the tree. It is so little compared to the giant bulk of the tree, and nobody can possibly identify who has chipped away what part of the trunk. When she has enough firewood for the next day, she slips away quietly into the night.

In the daylight it is easy to see the result of a thousand such visits by a score of village women. The trunk narrows down to a waist at a height of three to five feet above ground. Then, after a few months or perhaps a year or two, the tree begins to die. When the tree is dead, it is fair game for everybody, and many scarred stumps line the roads. Nobody can blame anybody because it is not any one person but everybody who has killed the tree—at least all the really poor.

Fortunately, there is a new scheme now, and it seems to be working. The government is helping the villagers to plant special fast-growing firewood trees, and paying for the watering and protection of these tree plantations until they are ready to provide fuel for the village cooking.

Outside of India I have seen another drama of trees and soil and water and human starvation working its tragic sequence that so often seems inevitable. This drama is unfolding in Ethiopia.

I first saw Ethiopia at the beginning of the nineteen-sixties when I went to Addis Ababa on behalf of the International Society for the Rehabilitation of the Disabled. My task was to negotiate the establishment of an all-Africa training center for leprosy workers, with an emphasis on rehabilitation. I had to meet the emperor Haile Selassie and his minister of health as well as ministers of agriculture and commerce, and the dean of the university medical college, which was just beginning. I also met representatives of American AID and the Rockefeller Foundation. Later, when the new training center was established, I went to work there. My job was surgery; I was teaching reconstruction of the hand and foot. But, as has happened so often in my life, it was the trees and the soil and agriculture that caught my attention. This was partly because most of our patients were farmers, and their future had to be in farming if they were not to be dislocated from their families and villages.

The emperor was very gracious as we talked about the problem, and he allowed our patients to farm tracts of the Royal Lands. The Swedish churches had sent farmers into Ethiopia to teach the patients how to farm more efficiently, and it was a joy to see acres of *tef*, the local food grain, growing to harvest. Patients with leprosy were learning how to work without damaging their insensitive hands. We were grateful to the benevolent old emperor; all seemed to be going well. Gradually, however, we began to see the real problems of that tragic country. When we visited distant treatment centers, we camped along the way, and we were impressed by the way the countryside was fissured with deep canyons where streams had eroded the soil on their way to join the Blue Nile. That mighty river flowed from Lake Tana through the deepest canyon of all on its way to Egypt and the Mediterranean Sea. Farmers on the edges of these canyons were having to retreat year by year as their soil slipped away into the rivers. Once there had been trees and forests on this land, but the trees had been felled for timber and firewood, and to make way for grazing and cultivation.

What impressed me most, however, were the poor crops and stony fields that were cultivated by the peasant farmers. Every field seemed to be covered with great stones and boulders. Many of these stones could rather easily have been levered up and rolled away to the edges of the fields, where they would have made walls to hold the soil in and keep marauders out. It did not take much inquiry to find out why such simple improvements had never been made, and why the peasants put up with the constant irritation of having to till and harvest between these rocks. They knew, and were frank to tell us, that if ever they made their fields look good, they would lose them. The ruling race of Amharas, based in the capital city, included all the lawyers and leaders of the country. An Amhara could claim any good piece of land simply by stating that it had belonged to his ancestors. Supporting documents were easy to obtain. In court the peasant had no chance. Thus his only hope of being allowed to continue farming his land was to make it appear worthless.

Both the Ford Foundation and the Rockefeller Foundation had considered sending help to teach good farming methods and to halt erosion, but both insisted to the emperor that land reform had to come first. Only if the land were owned by the people who farmed it would it be taken care of in a way that would preserve it for generations to come. The peasants had to have confidence that their handful of mud would still be there for their children. If not, why not let it be washed down into the river?

The emperor tried to introduce land reform, but he failed. The Amharas were too strong for him. The established church, the old Ethiopian Orthodox Church of which the emperor was head, had a vested interest in the status quo, and so was on the wrong side of real justice. This has happened often in the past when churches have gotten comfortable and wealthy.

On a state visit to Egypt the emperor walked down to the banks of the River Nile. He kneeled to scoop up two handfuls of the rich, fertile mud and raised his hands. "My country," he said. The Blue Nile had carried Ethiopia to Egypt, and the old emperor knew it. He could not send the mud upstream again, and he did not have the courage to make the changes that would have arrested further loss.

Today Emperor Selassie is dead. Every cabinet minister with whom I negotiated for our training center is dead. They were killed by the firing squads of the Revolution. I loved some of those men. Ato Abebe Retta, the Minister of Health, was a courteous gentleman of culture, and he had good plans for medical education. I enjoyed meals with him in his home, and we talked about leprosy control. He and the minister of agriculture were blindfolded and shot by a firing squad. The emperor, who gave us all that land—that regal figure who was the first president of the Organization of African Unity and who presided at the opening of our training center—died in prison. I could weep for them, but if I do, can I at the same time weep for the hundreds of thousands of peasants who are dying at this very moment because of famine? There might not have been a famine today if the trees had not all been cut down, if the land had not eroded away, if the absentee landlords of Ethiopia had not been so greedy, and if the church had insisted that justice should prevail. I did not like the Revolution or the foreign invaders who brought it about, but they would never have succeeded if the people had not been laboring under a sense of injustice. Ethiopia was ready for revolution. The new Marxist government has not succeeded in bringing back the trees or the land, and it has spent its energy in war. But the roots of Ethiopia's problems stem from generations ago, before the time of the leaders who recently died for their collective sins.

Today I live in Louisiana. I still treat leprosy patients and encourage them to get back to their homes and to their independence. On my land I have no soil problem, no tree problem, and no water problem. My topsoil is so deep and so rich that I would not even try to plumb its depth. The land is so flat that even when it floods, my soil stays where it is. Maybe I could grow vegetables, and live happily, at peace.

But I cannot be at peace. My home is right beside the mighty Mississippi River. I could probably throw a stone into the water from my roof. It used to be that every year the river would flood. My house is an old one, set up on piles, because at the time it was built, the occupants would expect to sit on their porch and watch the muddy waters of the Mississippi swirl under the house for a few days each year. If I were to analyze my garden soil, I know I would find that most of it came from Kansas and Ohio and Iowa and other states upriver. A farmer from Iowa could come to my garden, as the emperor of Ethiopia went to the banks of the Nile in Egypt, and scoop up a handful of mud and say "My farm."

But no mud comes from Iowa to my garden now, because the Corps of Engineers has built a dam, or levee, along the banks of the Mississippi, so the mud runs straight out to sea. During the spring floods I walk along the levee and look at the mud. They tell me that entire farms flow past my house every hour. I know that Iowa has lost more than half its topsoil just in the hundred or so years since people began farming that land. I feel rather proud of the fact that the people of India have been farming for three thousand years, and still have topsoil left. That is the legacy of an unbroken chain of grandfathers. It is Tata and his Tata that have preserved India's soil. Thank God they did not have agribusiness and big farm machines in those days.

Because I am haunted by the mountains of India and Nepal and by the erosion of Ethiopia, I have to ask why American farmers still lose soil. They tell me they know all about contour plowing, but they do not do it because modern farming machinery is so big that it is impossible or uneconomic to plow around contours. They just plow straight up and down. They lose the soil much faster, but they get the job done faster. This gives better returns to the shareholders, and improves all the market indicators. Shareholders and members of the board are today's absentee landlords of the farm. The farmers tell me that only small family farms still do contour plowing, but they are going out of business, and big oil companies like Tennaco are buying them up so they can use "efficient" farming methods and sell more oil in the process.

I am told that in America forests are replanted after they are cut down, and I think that is probably true, but I also understand that wide clear-cutting is practiced even on steep slopes, and that it is a matter of pride that every part of every tree is "used" for timber or pulp or chipboard when it is cut down. In other words, nothing goes back into the land. There is no building up of the soil, only depletion.

Now my Mississippi River is also the site of scores of petrochemical plants and herbicide factories. The proximity of the river makes it so convenient to use; it provides water for cooling towers and a place to dump effluents. I have plants to the left of me and plants to the right of me, upriver and downriver. Allied Chemical moved in a few years ago. It did not cut down many trees; it did not have to. Within a few years, all the trees downwind of the plant turned white and died. They tell me it was fluorides, but it could have been any one of the many effluents that blow off and foul our air. Louisiana has the highest incidence of cancer in the country. Eight years ago all the cattle in this area were declared to be unfit to sell for beef because unacceptable levels of tetrachlormethane were found in their fat. The chemical was traced back to an effluent from one of the petrochemical plants. I wonder what the levels are in me and my children. . . .

I look at the great Mississippi and think back to the days of Huckleberry Finn and his raft, when the river was largely water and fish. I look down now at the swirling mud, and I see it as no better than the Blue Nile, than the Cauvery River in India, which carries mud from the Nilgiri Hills, than the Ganges and the Brahmaputra, which carry the soil of Nepal and the Himalayas out into the Gulf of Bengal. Is there any common thread that links all of them together? It is not ignorance in all cases. It is sometimes dire poverty that leads to the cutting down of the trees. There would be enough for all if it were not for another common thread, and that is greed. More profit. Faster returns on investments. A bigger share *for me* of what is available now but may not be available tomorrow.

I would gladly give up medicine and surgery tomorrow if by so doing I could have some influence on policy with regard to mud and soil. The world will die from lack of soil and pure water long before it will die from lack of antibiotics or surgical skill and knowledge. But what can be done if the destroyers of our earth know what they are doing, and do it still? What can be done if people really believe that free enterprise has to mean an absolute lack of restraint on those who have no care for the future?

All is not lost if there are still people who have faith and people who care. God still has a church that produces people who care. In the final analysis it is not knowledge or lack of it that makes a difference, but concerned people. A sense of concern for the earth is still transmitted by person-to-person communication and by personal example better than by any other method. Old Tata still lives on. He lives in the boys who played in the mud, and they will pass on his concern for the soil and his sense of the importance of it for future generations. Old Mr. Fritschi still lives on. The love of trees that he tried to promote in the Nilgiri Hills is now being promoted by his son, Ernest, on the plains of Karagiri. This is the place that I love to visit because I get a sense that the earth is being revived. If it can happen in one place, then why not everywhere? A single dedicated person giving a good example is better than much wringing of hands and a prophecy of doom.

Ernest grew to love India, and he became a citizen and married a lovely Indian woman. He studied at Madras University and became a doctor, then an orthopedic surgeon. Working with leprosy patients, he joined the leprosy mission and worked in many countries, including Ethiopia. Eventually he became director of the Schieffelin Research and Training Center at Karagiri, near Vellore.

The land for the center was once barren gravel, with not a tree anywhere, and water was hard to locate. I remember walking over the large acreage before we started to build on it and thinking that it was no surprise that the government had donated it so freely, since it was good for nothing else. But Ernest had faith in the land and was determined to prove that it could be productive of more than buildings and a hospital. Other directors had made a good start, but Ernest made a rule for himself that every year he would plant trees and more trees. To follow his rule, he collected seeds and seedlings from everywhere and nourished them in his own garden until they were strong. Then he planted them just before the rains, and had them watered by staff and patients until they had root systems deep enough to survive. The hill that formed one border of the Karagiri land was bare and rocky, and the rains would send a rushing flood of water over the gravel of the hospital grounds. So Ernest built contour ridges of gravel and soil that held the water long enough for it to soak in.

I remember the hospital and the staff houses and chapel that grew up around it. They were gray and white and stood out against the skyline. They were the only structures to break the monotony of the gravel slopes for miles. When I approach that hospital today, it is invisible, hidden in a forest that is higher than the tallest buildings. The place has been declared a sanctuary by the Environmental Department of the government. The whole area is full of birds; we counted and identified about forty species in one afternoon. The water table, which is falling in most places, was rising last year under the gravel at Karagiri. Soil is being built up, not lost.

What are a few lush acres among the million barren ones? It is important to me because it sounds a message: one man can make a difference. Dedication is what is needed, and faith. It is important, too, because the man who brought about this little revolution is not a professional farmer or a government official. He is simply a doctor who loves trees and soil and water. He was sometimes criticized by his board of directors, who said that his goal and objectives should be to treat leprosy patients and help rehabilitate them. Money should not be diverted to other goals like farming and reforestation. But Ernest has proved that concern for soil and trees benefits patients too. Buildings do not need to be air-conditioned when they are shaded by trees. Patients who see and participate in good practices on the land learn to reproduce these practices when they go home.

Not far away is the Vellore Christian Medical College, founded by the beloved American doctor Ida S. Scudder. She loved trees, and she insisted on building the college on an extensive piece of land where there would be room for growth and breath and gardens and trees. She was followed by others who had the same view. The first Indian director was also a woman, Dr. Hilda Lazerus. She doubtless had claims to fame in her own medical specialty, but I remember her for her love of trees. From time to time she would go on inspection tours around all the buildings, including the staff houses. All waste water from basins and baths was discharged over the ground outside the houses by separate waste pipes from each sink or basin. Hilda Lazerus always spotted the waste pipe that was without a tree or a vegetable plot to nourish. She would call up any householder, even a senior professor in the college, and would insist that a papaya tree be planted to use the waste water from the pipe. The next day a seedling or even just a seed would be delivered to his door.

Hilda Lazerus is long gone, but her trees remain, and her philosophy remains too. The doctors who received their training at Vellore are teaching their undernourished patients that they can stay well by using every drop of water to grow plants and fruit trees. The same philosophy has guided new outreach developments in public health and community medicine that are an important part of the work of the college. In my day we used to get excited and concerned about new drugs and new diagnostic equipment, but today when I visit, I find that the director of RHUSA, a center for community health, is more likely to be excited about preserving the water table, growing the right kinds of crops, and preserving the soil. This is health, and this is hope for the future, because the students who graduate from this college go all over India, and they go with concern for trees and water because they know that that is how life is sustained. I love to return to Vellore every year. It tells me that all is not lost, and that each of us can make a difference. There is still life in the land, and God still blesses those who recognize that "the earth is the Lord's."

I am a grandfather now. My grandchildren do not call me Tata, but I rather wish they would. It would not mean much to them, but it would remind me that in addition to the immortality of the spirit, we all have a kind of immortality of the flesh. If the children called me Tata, it would remind me that, down through the centuries, there may be many generations of people who will bear my humanity and who will enjoy life or who will suffer in proportion to the care that I now take to preserve the good gifts that God has given to us. Part of that care is exercised in teaching and in example. My grandson is called Daniel, and the next time he comes to visit me, I shall take him out into my garden and I shall scoop up a handful of mud I shall ask him, "Daniel, what is this?"